Christmas
with
Southern Living®
1983

Jo Voce and Shelley Stewart

Oxmoor House, Inc. Birmingham

Copyright© 1983 by Oxmoor House, Inc.
Book Division of Southern Progress Corporation
P.O. Box 2463, Birmingham, Alabama 35201

Library of Congress Number: 81-80138

ISBN: 0-8487-0543-2
Manufactured in the United States of America
First Printing

Contents

Introduction

It is almost time again. To put up the tree and decorate it with new ornaments and all the ones saved from past years. To hang a wreath on the door as a greeting to all who pass by. To arrange a new decoration for the table, the buffet, the mantel—all around the house. To invite friends for coffee and dessert. To give a special gift with a personal touch. It is almost time to welcome Christmas into our homes and to share it with our family and friends. We hope that you will begin the festive season with the inspiration of new designs and practical instructions from *Christmas with Southern Living 1983*.

"Christmas around the South" is a wonderful photographic sampler of celebrations and decorations; indoors and out, the preparations for the holiday season are influenced by the history and the materials of the region. "Decorating for the Holidays" offers dozens of ideas for new decorations and instructions for making some traditional holiday favorites. A "Christmas Bazaar" is filled with gift ideas—a card basket to cross-stitch, a new stocking to crochet, ornaments to needlepoint, a gentle lamb to sew, a teddy bear and a jumping jack to cut from wood, ornaments to paint on foil, and doves and favorbaskets to make from organdy. There are also wraps and projects for children. "Celebrations from the Kitchen" has new recipes for sharing at home and for packaging as gifts. Make lists and check them twice in the "Christmas Journal," where there is room for card lists, size charts, gift lists, and all the events you need to record on a calendar. Patterns—full-sized and ready to trace—are given for projects that need them.

Plan ahead, make ahead, and when it is time for the holidays, you will be prepared to enjoy the season with your home all ready, your gifts made, and the recipes chosen for the good times to share with your loved ones. Merry Christmas!

Christmas around the South

ll across the South, the season is proclaimed with decorations, pageants, and special displays. With Christmas lights and some ingenuity, a skyscraper in Birmingham and a boat in Fort Lauderdale are turned into holiday displays. A Christmas tree is drawn in lights across the facade of a house in Dallas. Candles glow in the windows along Tenth Avenue in Gastonia, North Carolina.

The natural materials of different parts of the South are made into decorations for indoor and outdoor use. *Ristras* of chili peppers are shaped into wreaths in Texas, and small sweet-grass baskets become tree ornaments in Charleston.

From a Florida cabin, there is a candleholder that would be perfectly suitable on a mantel in a contemporary home.

From Old Salem, there are eighteenth-century "illuminations"—delicately colored pictures of Bible stories that become translucent when candles are placed behind them. Dollhouses of all sorts and sizes are decorated for the season in a display from the Anniston Museum of Natural History.

Join us in discovering the joys of Christmas all around the South—in large cities and in small towns, in public events and in quiet contemplation. We would enjoy hearing from you about displays and decorations in your area of the South.

Charleston Accents

Charleston, South Carolina, is a city at ease with itself and its traditions. Charlestonians speak with an accent that is almost as distinguishable from other Southern accents as it is from Yankee talk. The flower women, a Charleston tradition of long standing, can be found all year long in the same place, selling flowers in summer and wreaths of greenery and vines in the winter. Among their wares are sweet-grass baskets, made from the grass that grows near the marshes.

In the past few years, sweet grass has become the basis for Christmas tree ornaments. Designed by members of The Garden Club, the small baskets, bells, and stars are made by the flower women and decorated by club members. Sold through an annual sale that benefits the gardens of the Manigault House, the ornaments provide a distinct Charleston accent for a Christmas tree. Shown here are two trees decorated with the ornaments. In a small bed-and-breakfast inn of the historic waterfront district (named, appropriately, The Sweet Grass Inn), sweet-grass ornaments and plaid bows fill a tree (left). On another tree, in a private home, the sweet-grass ornaments are used as part of a melánge of varied decorations (far right).

The Manigault House, built in 1803 in the Adam style, is a museum house of The Charleston Museum. Decorated for Christmas by The Garden Club of Charleston, the distinguished house is graciously accented with decorations of greenery and other accents from nature. From its own gardens come camellias for the dining room—arranged in a handsome silver centerpiece made in London in 1816. On the windows of the dining room hang wreaths of balsam with sprigs of variegated ivy and poinsettias (in florist's vials). In the library, a wreath of red cedar is dressed with the blossoms and fruit of the sago palm and with the nut of the tung tree.

5

From a Cracker Cabin

In a log cabin at Morningside Nature Farm in Gainesville, Florida, holiday decorations reflect the simple lifestyle of the 1840s. "Cracker" is a term used fondly to define rural families in north-central Florida. The one-room house with a sleeping loft is set in a sandy clearing—a practical consideration in the flat, pine-timbered land that was periodically subject to natural brush fires. Inside the cabin, the decorations are made from found objects. The tree is a small pine decorated with strings of popcorn and bits of ribbon and yarn.

On the wooden mantel, pine branches and candleholders from twigs bid welcome to a warm and friendly fireside.

Imagine several of the candleholders, with their simple and functional shapes, clustered on the mantel in a contemporary family room. To make the twig candleholder, cut a 3-pronged twig, attach a round from a larger twig with a nail, and set a votive candle in place with a drop of wax.

In Old Salem

Old Salem is a restored area that functions as a living museum in the center of Winston-Salem, North Carolina. The town of Salem was settled by a group of Moravians who fled the religious turmoil of Central Europe in the eighteenth century. The city of Winston was begun just to the north and eventually surrounded Salem.

Today, Christmas in Old Salem reflects simpler times and the religious heritage of the settlers: the smell of freshly baked breads and cookies, wreaths of greenery on doorways and windows, and music from a brass band.

Perhaps the most treasured decorations are the "illuminations" preserved from the eighteenth century. Originally teaching aids used in the Moravian Church, they are pictures painted on thin paper and placed in front of a candle so that they become translucent.

Lights of Gastonia

Along Tenth Avenue in Gastonia, North Carolina, each window that faces the street glows with the light of a single electrified candle. The candles of Gastonia are a tradition dating to the 1930s when wax candles were used. Electrified candles were soon on the market, however, and these were easier to maintain. Now a city-wide tradition, the candles can be seen in the windows in most residential neighborhoods.

Christmas Lights & Night Skies

Thomas Alva Edison invented the electric light bulb in October of 1879. By December of 1882, the vice president of Edison's electric company had a lighted tree in his home. Eighty lights (about the size of walnuts and in red, white, and blue) were strung on a tree. Ever since, Christmas lights in bright colors have broken the darkness of night skies.

In Birmingham, Alabama, the skyline becomes a giant Christmas card as the lights are turned on in the First National-Southern Natural Building. To create the designs, red- and green-colored sleeves are slipped over 2700 fluorescent tubes that form the perimeter lights of the building and are located between windows and blinds. When the lights go on (from dark until midnight, mid-December until December 31), the sleeves are illuminated along the window panels and produce the designs.

A Christmas tree is silhouetted on a house in the Highland Park section of Dallas, Texas. To draw the tree so symmetrically would be fairly easy if the house were as small as the photograph—but the house is large, the drawing materials are strings of lights, and the working position must have been on a ladder. Our compliments to the person who strung the lights.

Boat parades are Florida's contribution to the seasonal display of Christmas lights against winter skies. Shown here are boats from the Fort Lauderdale Parade, during which the boats cruise ten miles up the Intercoastal Waterway. Other boat parades are held in Deland, Madeira Beach, and Pompano Beach.

Celebrations in Miniature

In Anniston, Alabama, an annual Christmas exhibition of dollhouses at the Anniston Museum of Natural History has become a favorite with children—and grown-ups too. The dollhouses are varied: a fire station, a log cabin, a mouse house, and dollhouses of various ages and styles. The Santa workshop, shown below, is of Norwegian origin.

Other photographs show the decoration of one dollhouse. In the bedroom at right (where a doily is a canopy and another is pressed into service as a rug), tiny gifts are wrapped and ready for giving. A collection of miniatures is used in an upstairs sitting room (below right). In the dining room (top, page 11), toothpicks have become candles, old earrings are transformed into table decorations, and buttons are plates. In the living room (bottom, page 11), "gold" charms are the Christmas toys.

While you are in the museum, be sure to see the Heath Hen, Eskimo Curlew, Passenger Pigeon, and Carolina Parakeet—all extinct. They are a part of the Werner-Regar Bird Collection made by Pennsylvania naturalist William Werner about the time of the Civil War.

Note to children: Don't miss the elephant and the Baobab tree.

Red Hot Peppers

How hot? Texas hot. Chili peppers are grown, of course, for culinary purposes, but the *ristras* are easily curled into a wreath for the holidays. Shown here: a single chili pepper, harvesting the peppers, and red hot holiday wreaths.

Decorating for the Holidays

rim the tree. Hang a wreath. Lay logs for a cozy fire. Light the candles. Inside and out, there are so many things to do—all of them a challenge to the excitement of the holiday and the creativity that it fosters. Christmas adds a seasonal note to Southern hospitality as we open our homes and draw people into our lives. In "Decorating for the Holidays," you will find bright ideas and complete instructions for all manner of new decorations that will add beauty to your surroundings.

For outside, make an extravagantly sized Walk-Through Wreath or a more sedate Della Robbia Wreath. Or try a living ivy wreath and another made with crab shells. For indoors, there are ornaments: vividly painted fish, pinecones made into flowers and poodles, and felt "cookies." Instructions are given for making favorite traditional decorations like fruit pyramids, and brand new designs for organdy favor-baskets and gentle doves will help to set a party table.

For decorations that smell as good as they look, try the Apple Rings or the Cookie Candle-holders. Make a table skirt from Christmas fabrics and top the table with a collection of frames for favorite holiday photographs. Cluster family memorabilia on a wreath that is as individual as your family's memories are. Indoor wreaths can be made of rabbit tobacco and red peppers or from moss. A Victorian Tree under Glass will accent an entry hall.

There are other ideas—toys arranged under the tree if the gifts are not wrapped, ways to make your holiday table sparkle, accents for the mantel or a shelf.

Spruce up the Outside

Walk-Through Wreath

Begin a party—or a season—with an entry through this spectacular walk-through wreath. On a backing of plywood, the wreath is sturdy enough to support greenery, lights, and ribbon. The plywood form can be saved from year to year. The possible variations in greenery are quite numerous. The greenery shown here is gathered from a Christmas tree lot; next year, the wreath could be made with magnolia leaves.

MATERIALS:

2 sheets ¼" plywood of marine quality (1 sheet if you are willing to piece two of the four quarter-circles)
24 (¾"-long) stove bolts
drill and bits
dark green spray paint (outdoor)
greenery
staples and staple gun
nails
outdoor Christmas lights
outdoor ribbon for bow (about 6 yards)

You will need a piece of paper or cardboard large enough for drawing a circle that is eight feet in diameter. Paper can be taped together to make a large piece.

Draw a circle 8' in diameter on the paper. Draw another circle that is 6'4" in diameter inside the first. This will give you a wreath shape that is 10" wide. (Figure 1.) Cut the pattern in four equal parts. (Figure 2.)

Place the four pattern pieces on the plywood, and mark the edges. Cut the plywood to shape.

Using scrap plywood, cut 4 splicing joiners that are 12" x 6". Drill 6 holes in each joiner and 3 holes in the ends of the pieces of the circle for the bolts. Bolt and join all parts. (Figure 3.) Make any adjustments necessary. (Small cracks and irregularities will be covered with greenery.)

Spray paint the form dark green on all sides. Allow to dry.

Gather greenery. Cut into 15" to 24" lengths and staple to the plywood, attaching each cluster in the same direction around the form so new clusters overlap stapled ends. Extend greenery 4" to 6" on inside and outside of plywood form.

Raise the wreath into place; this requires more than one set of hands. Determine an adequate support against the house for the wreath; this will vary from house to house. For safety, the wreath should be nailed securely in place; remember that this is the season for wind.

After the frame is nailed securely to the house, place outdoor lights on the wreath and add a huge bow.

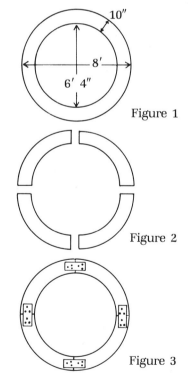

Figure 1

Figure 2

Figure 3

14

Cut five (5") lengths from the wide ends of the selloum spathes and soak a few hours or overnight in water.

Remove from water and spread each petal with the fingers, retaining the curves and rough edges. Thread the five petals onto a 10"-long piece of smooth, firm wire, with the wire about an inch from the bottom. To reduce the bulk, trim away the square edges, tapering the base of each petal but leaving enough to hold securely. (Figure 1.)

Prepare the stamen and the stem by placing the stem of seeds (or other stamen) against an inch or two of the heavier wire and taping the two firmly together. With pliers, draw the petals firmly together. Fasten tightly together, winding the wire to make a base. (Figure 2.) Spread the petals and insert the stem and stamen through the center, so that the stem will be inside and the wire will go through the base.

Finish the flower by covering the wired base with brown florist's tape. Extend the tape onto the stem, but leave the lower part of the stem smooth so the flower can be more easily inserted into an arrangement. While the petals are still moist, arrange them as desired. Attach clothespins to hold them in position. Stand flower in a jar to dry. (Figure 3.)

From Nature's Bounty

Shape spathes of selloum (split-leaf philodendron) into graceful "hibiscus" to top a wreath. In this wreath of subtle colors but strong shapes, pine straw on a coat hanger base is held in place with a wrapping of raffia, and pinecones finish the design.

FOR THE FLOWER

MATERIALS:
    5 dried spathes of selloum
    1 seed stem, stick of cinnamon or other "found" stamen
    10" (#20) smooth wire
    5 or more inches (#16 or heavier) smooth wire
    brown florist's tape

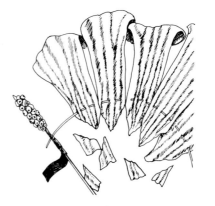

Figure 1   Figure 2

FOR THE WREATH

MATERIALS:
  many long pine needles
  raffia
  a coat hanger
  #40 binding wire
  brown tape
  pinecones
  3 "hibiscus" flowers

Pull the coat hanger into a circle to give form and strength for your wreath. Wind the hook with tape to form a hanger for the wreath.

Do not separate the needles from their base that holds them together. Gather a handful of needles, turning them in the same direction. Starting at the hook, bind the needles to the wire with raffia. Continue around the circle, turning the needles in the same direction. Make a second round, and, finally, a third round. Tie and bind as tightly as possible.

Fasten the hibiscus flowers at the top of the wreath with covered wire (#40 binding wire covered with brown tape). Wire cones to the wreath in a pleasing arrangement. Cones from white pine are used on the wreath shown here, but others would be suitable.

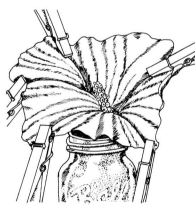

Figure 3

Wreath of Living Ivy

This wreath will last and last—because the ivy is rooted and growing in a base of moss. Make living ivy wreaths for friends; they are sure to enjoy them throughout the winter season.

MATERIALS:
  2 wire wreath forms, 12″ or 14″ in
    diameter
  sheet moss
  fine wire
  rooted ivy
  heavy wire for loop

Fill one of the wire wreath forms with sheet moss, packing in as much as you possibly can. Cover with the other wreath form, and use the fine wire to wrap securely. Twist ends of wire, so wreath forms are carefully fastened together. Soak the wreath base you have just made in water until the moss is wet. Using a pencil, poke holes in the moss, and stick the rooted ivy in the holes. Fill as full of ivy as you like. Wrap a heavy wire around the wreath and form into a loop for hanging.

17

To make the vine wreath, select several long, thick vines. Beginning with the thicker end of one vine, loop the vine into a circle about 16" in diameter. Add another loop to the circle, pulling the vine through and around the first loop in a long spiral. Continue to add loops, pulling the vine through the circle in spirals that secure the shape. Add as many vines as you need to complete a wreath, tucking the ends of the vines into the structure of the wreath.

Loop wire through a hole in each of the sand dollars and wire to wreath. Punch holes in underside of the crab shells by gently twisting an ice pick into the shell, push wire through holes, and wire to wreath. Gather short twigs into a small cluster, wire together, and attach at top of wreath. Gather longer twigs into a cluster, wire together, and attach at bottom of wreath. Make a bow from the ribbon, and wire it in place at bottom of wreath. Slip sprigs of cedar behind the bow. Finally, wedge the scallop and snail shells between loops of vines.

Low Country Wreath

Remember balmy afternoon walks along the shore and through the woods with this gathering of shells and twigs. Dwellers of coastal areas will appreciate the soft peach shades of crab shells, the bleached whites of sand dollars and snails, and the subtle grays of scallops against the texture of a vine wreath.

MATERIALS:
  vines for making wreath
  5 crab shells, bleached
  2 sand dollars
  2 scallop shells
  2 snail shells
  lichen-covered twigs
  sprigs of cedar
  4 yards outdoor ribbon for bow
  florist's wires

Tree of Pinecones

Espaliered against a screen, this tree of cones stands beside the doorway to an enclosed patio. The tree is approximately 4' tall and 3' wide at the bottom. The appearance changes as the cones close in rainy weather and open when the sun shines brightly.

MATERIALS:
  wooden bucket
  scrap of ¼" plywood
  scrap wood
  drill and bits
  wire in various gauges
  brown florist's tape
  pinecones (4" to 6" in length)
  florist's wire
  wood glue
  purchased red birds

Select a wooden bucket that is in proportion to the height of the tree that you plan; exact measurements are less important than the general appearance. Saw the bucket in half vertically. Place half-bucket on plywood, draw around the outside, and cut the plywood to form a back. Tack and glue the back to the bucket half. Insert a block of scrap wood at center back of bucket and glue to plywood backing. Drill a hole at top center of wood block; the center wire will be inserted into this hole after the tree is assembled. (Figure 1.)

Select a heavy center wire (similar in thickness to a coat hanger) about 4' long. This will be the trunk of the tree. Make a loop at the top of the trunk wire; this will be used for hanging. Branch wires can be about half as heavy as the trunk wire, but they should be rigid enough to support the cones without drooping. Cut wires for branches, cutting to decreasing lengths as limbs are nearer the top of the tree. Wrap the wires with brown florist's tape.

Sort pine cones and use larger ones near bottom of tree and smaller ones near top.

Twist a florist's wire 1½ times around a pinecone near the base, pull the wire to the base of the cone, and twist the ends of the wire together. (Figure 2.) Wire about 8 cones for a bottom limb. Twist the wires from the cones around a branch wire, attaching the cones as shown. (Figure 3.)

Twist the wire of the branch around the main trunk wire, using pliers to tighten. Continue to add branches, shortening the limbs as you near the top of the tree.

Insert the trunk into the hole in the wood block; glue securely.

Wire purchased birds to the tree.

A method for mounting the tree will be determined by the specific spot where the tree will be

used. Plastic filament can form a hanging loop through the hook at the top of the tree and the base can be nailed in place; other arrangements will be determined by where the tree is used.

The tree can be stored in a large flat box and saved to be used again and again.

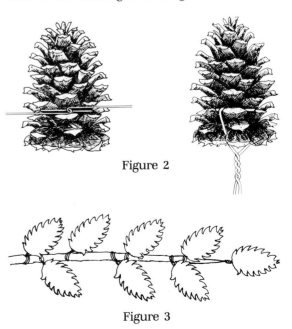

Figure 2

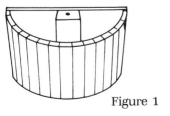

Figure 1

Figure 3

Della Robbia Wreaths, Southern Style

The aristocrats of wreaths, "Della Robbias" add the colors and contours of fruit to bases of evergreen. Fruit was plentiful in the Southern colonies, so it was naturally used in Christmas decorations. Mounds of fruit were heaped in the centers of tables; after dinner, guests helped themselves to a bit of the centerpiece. There were few materials available to enhance basic green wreaths, so fruit was added for color.

Colonial restorations, such as Colonial Williamsburg, often use these historically authentic wreaths in decorations for the season. In an area where a number of della robbias are used, it can be quite interesting to observe the variety of designs.

In addition to fruit, other items with sculptural shapes are often added. Pinecones, deodar cones, dried okra, nuts, clusters of berries, dried plants in contrasting colors—all of these can be used in the design of wreaths.

These wreaths have advantages for city dwellers who have only limited access to natural greenery. A purchased wreath of greenery can be made an individual design with the addition of fruit and nuts from the grocery and a few cones that will last and last.

Plan your wreath for the 12 days of Christmas. Even in the best of climates, the fruit cannot be expected to last through an extended season. If you keep your decorations in place for a lengthy period, substitute cones and pods that are sculptural in nature, or plan to replace the fruit as needed.

SELECT A BASE

Choose either a large wire wreath form or a straw wreath form. If you choose to use the rigid wire base, plan to wire the greenery to the base with a spool of flexible wire. To attach greenery to the straw wreath form, you will need U-shaped florist's pins.

To hold the shape with the weight of the fruit, the wreath base must be quite strong. Two straw wreath forms from the same source can vary in strength. Stabilize the form by wrapping it with additional twine, looping the twine over and through the wreath form. If the straw form is wrapped in strips of green plastic, it will be less noticeable behind a base of greenery.

ATTACH THE GREENERY

Greenery of many types can be used. Choose from magnolia, aucuba, ligustrum, pine, boxwood, holly, and cedar. Or mix several types of greenery in a single wreath. Trimmings from a Christmas tree are an excellent background.

If you cut your greenery from shrubbery, prune with care. Pine, juniper, and arborvitae are not hurt by winter cuttings, but care should be taken not to cut too many branches from the same area or the shape may be permanently lopsided. From rhododendron, laurel, or andromeda, take only two years' growth—count two joints from the tip of a branch and cut on the side of the joint nearest the tip of the branch. From yew, boxwood, and Japanese holly, take only short clippings so that you do not expose tender growth that is used to the protection of the outer leaves. Condition greenery by placing it in water overnight so that it soaks up as much water as possible.

Cut greenery into small sprigs. Wire several sprigs together with the wire of a florist's pick. As the small bunches are attached to the wreath base, all the greenery should be in the same direction as it circles the wreath. The ends of each new piece should cover the stems of the previous cluster.

Use a spool of flexible wire to attach the greenery to a wire base, catching the florist's picks as you wrap the spool around both wreath and picks. If you are using a straw wreath form, use the U-shaped pins to attach the clusters of greenery to the base.

On a base of greenery, apples and lemons are combined with berries and three kinds of pinecones.

Symmetrical positioning of pineapples at the bottom of this wreath establishes the formal design of the wreath.

ATTACH FRUIT, PODS, & CONES

Fruit can vary from yellow lemons to bright oranges to green pears to red apples. Add pomegranates and kumquats. (Bananas do not last well and should not be used.)

Fruit-laden wreaths can be quite symmetrical, but they are just as attractive when the fruit is irregularly spaced. Fruit can be attached in clusters, or single pieces can be spaced around the wreath.

Fruit is quite heavy and must be attached carefully so it does not fall from the wreath. To attach fruit to a wire wreath form, you must wire the fruit. To do this, push a piece of florist's wire through the fruit and twist the wires together. (Figure 1.) Then twist the wires to the wreath form.

To attach fruit to a straw wreath form, you also need a florist's pick. After you have wired the fruit, make a hole in the fruit with the sharp end of a pick. Reverse the pick and push the blunt end into the fruit, and twist the wires tightly around the pick. (Figure 2.) (Never eat fruit that has been punctured by the picks; the dye in the pick can be poisonous.) Push the pick into the straw wreath form, and, if necessary, add a florist's pin across the pick.

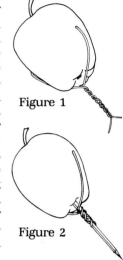

Figure 1

Figure 2

Add seedpods from okra or milkweed, pinecones turned in various directions, and clusters of shiny red berries.

On a railing that is generously garlanded, this wreath has lemons, apples, and berries arranged asymmetrically.

Note that the large cones form a circle—all lying in the same direction around the wreath. Inside this circle, osage oranges are evenly spaced. An inside row of small cones completes the design.

23

WITH THE WREATH

Wreaths, as pretty as they are, can be even prettier when they are used with garlands and other decorative touches.

Pineapples, clusters of twigs, and a cheery plaid bow wired to light standards are a handsome addition as they flank the door on which the wreath is hung.

For a different accent, wire several pieces of fruit, leaving the wires a bit longer than for the wreath. Gather the pieces of fruit into a cluster, and twist the wires together. Add these to a garland by attaching at either side of the top of a doorway.

Special Touches for the House

Family Memory Wreaths

As families gather for Christmas, they celebrate not only the holiday itself but also the reunion of the family and the warmth, joy, and security of belonging to each other. These wonderful Family Memory Wreaths celebrate the best things in the life of the family. Little things too precious to throw away are made a part of the wreaths—the collection of memorabilia growing from year to year and always changing, welcoming new children and grandchildren, celebrating a major milestone in someone's life or just an afternoon walk in the woods.

And, yes, you can believe your eyes. There really are Easter eggs and spacemen on these Christmas wreaths. There are real keepsakes: firecrackers, earrings, scout badges. There are also miniatures to represent other events: dolls for children, small bagpipes for a Scottish ancestry, a small horse for a real pony. The miniatures are inexpensive—more often than not collected from dime store toy and party counters and given a coat of clear nail polish to preserve them.

Two versions of the Family Memory Wreath represent a larger family tradition. The older wreath (shown on page 26) is laden with the mementos of a couple, their children, and their grandchildren; the wreath has become so heavy that it requires a plywood support. The wreath at right belongs to a daughter of the owner of the older wreath. The two wreaths have some keepsakes in common, but there are also differences that reflect the diverging and converging of the lives of mother and daughter. Other grown children in the same family also have their own versions of the Family Memory Wreath. As each new Christmas season arrives, the wreaths are

brought out and hung again. Each wreath must be inspected carefully by family members and friends to see what has been added and to remember all the old tokens.

On the older wreath, you will find: A small manger scene surrounded by angels and a star. Big "50" souvenirs from a fiftieth wedding anniversary and from class reunions. Piano for children's lessons and all the trips to those lessons. Car keys for new cars. Easter eggs because a son's class hunted eggs each year from kindergarten through grade school in the family's yard. A set of pearl earrings worn to the weddings of all the children. A green worm for gardening. A cup from a child's tea set. A spaceman for the year that a man first walked on the moon. A number of party souvenirs from gatherings of a group called the Sewing Club—organized 30 years ago and still meeting once a month with the same eight members.

On the daughter's wreath, you will find: Rhinestone earrings from college days. Small dolls for each child. An apple for days as a teacher. Gingerbread for the tradition of making cookies together at Christmas. Boy Scout and Brownie insignias for children's activities—and doll-sized ballet shoes, a baseball mitt, tennis racket, and football. Brass bell that once adorned a cat's collar. The engine from a son's toy train. Bride and groom for a daughter's wedding.

TO MAKE A FAMILY WREATH

Whatever your family remembers with joy is worth commemorating. Place a straw form on plywood, and draw around the outside and inside of the form. Cut the backing. Place the straw wreath form on the plywood form, and wrap securely with twine. Wrap with strips of green plastic. Place artificial greenery around edges of wreath. Cover trinkets of metal with a coat of clear nail polish. Wrap souvenirs with the wires of florist's picks, and attach picks to wreath.

Cookies & More Cookies

Cookies have been a part of homemade decorations as long as there have been Christmas trees in this country. In the homes of colonial America, most of the cookies were eaten when the tree came down, but a few might be saved to use year after year—or as long as they lasted.

Making cookies to last has been a challenge to numerous cooks, and thrifty housewives have sometimes substituted cheaper materials. A combination of cornmeal and glue was one substitution for regular ingredients—just as contemporary cooks may use bread dough in ornaments that resemble cookies. The Victorians made fancy cookies by brushing the tops of cookies with egg white and pressing pretty Christmas pictures onto them.

The cookie tree shown here continues the tradition of making real cookies for the tree, and it also offers a new variation in the long succession of cookie substitutes. Made with the

27

same cookie cutters that are used for real cookies, stuffed felt ornaments are decorated with buttons, beads, and other trims to resemble cookies that come from the oven. Cutouts of felt are used to scatter cookies over a tree skirt—again using cookie cutters for patterns. The cookie cutters used in all the projects are currently available in most kitchen shops and department stores. If you cannot find these particular cutters, though, you can have a wonderful time making new designs with different ones.

TREE SKIRT

Even a small tree will be better dressed with an imaginative tree skirt. The skirt shown with the small tree measures only 36" in diameter, while the skirt shown with the large tree is a generous 52" in diameter. The plaid fabric can be found in wide widths, making it a good choice for cutting a large circle without the necessity of first piecing material.

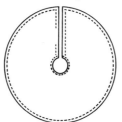

MATERIALS:
  wool-blend plaid fabric, 1½ yards (54"-wide) for large tree skirt or 1 yard (36"-wide) for small tree skirt
  red fabric for lining, 1½ yards (54"-wide) for large skirt or 1 yard (36"-wide) for small skirt
  thread to match
  ¼ yard each of felt in shades of tan and light brown
  squares of red, green, and gold felt
  beads, buttons, rickrack, and other notions

For the large tree skirt, cut a 54"-diameter circle of plaid and of lining fabric. For the small tree skirt, cut a 36"-diameter circle of plaid and lining fabric. For either size, mark a 5" circle in the middle of the lining. (You may find it helpful to read instructions for cutting a large circle on page 40.)

Place the two circles of fabric with right sides together. Sew around the outside edges and around the inside circle. Following the diagram at left, sew two lines 1" apart from outer seam to inner circle, leaving a segment of one line open for turning. Cut *between* the two straight seam lines and around the *inside* of the small circle. Clip the inside curves around the small circle. Turn the skirt right side out, press, and whip-stitch the opening. Topstitch around all edges of tree skirt.

To make the cookies, place cookie cutters on felt; draw around them with a pencil. Cut just inside the pencil lines, so you remove the marks as you cut. Cut some rectangles for packages and some doughnut shapes for wreaths. Sew on beads, buttons, rickrack, and other notions to repeat the icing designs for cookies. To get started, look at the cookies on the cover and through the book—then improvise.

Lay the skirt flat, plaid side up. Arrange the cookies on the tree skirt, not following a particular pattern but filling spaces until the arrangement pleases you. Using a small amount of glue at several spots around the edge of each felt shape, glue the felt cookies in place. Allow to dry thoroughly.

REAL COOKIES FOR THE TREE

The cookies on the tree are from the same recipes as those shown on the cover and throughout the book. The recipes are given in Celebrations from the Kitchen, pages 84-91. To make the cookies last longer, there are several suggestions given here.

First, cut the cookies you plan to hang on the tree from thicker dough, about ¼" thick.

Make holes by pushing a plastic drinking straw through the cookies just as they come from the oven. Make the hole well inside the cookie; remember that the weight of the cookie will pull against the small area beside the hole. The end of the straw will deteriorate as you use it on hot cookies, so have scissors handy to snip a new end for the straw.

Use narrow ribbon to form loops for hanging; cord is too fine and will cut its way through the cookie.

After cookies are decorated, arrange them in single layers on pans or trays, and allow them to

set for several days to harden before they are hung on the tree.

Adults will probably enjoy looking at the tree as much as they would enjoy eating the cookies—but children may have very different ideas. To avoid losing the decorations to cookie thieves, keep a tray of cookies for eating handy. Or hide some small packages of cellophane-wrapped cookies beneath the tree to become tree favors.

Finally, accept the fact that some of the cookies are likely to break. Until only a few years ago, Christmas trees were kept up for only a short time; now, we keep them throughout a much longer holiday season. The longer the tree stays up, the more likely it is that some of the cookies will fall and break. Make extras for replacements, and don't waste a joyous holiday worrying about cookies that fall.

COOKIES FROM FELT

Use the same cookie cutters that you use for making real cookies. Large cutters with simple outlines will be the simplest to use. Decorate with beads, pearls, snips of felt, rickrack—all the notions that look like the sprinkles and decorations on the real cookies.

MATERIALS:
felt in shades of tan, light brown, red, gold, and green
sewing thread
polyester stuffing
beads, buttons, rickrack, and other trims

On a piece of felt, draw around the cutters with a pencil, leaving about ½" between all the shapes. Do not cut out the shapes.

Place another piece of felt beneath the one on which you have drawn the shapes. Adjust your machine for a straight stitch with a stitch length of 18-20 stitches an inch. Sew along the pencil marks that outline the designs, leaving an opening for turning along the straightest side of each of your designs. After you have sewn all the shapes, cut them apart. Trim each design very close (about ⅛") to the seam line. Turn; use a crochet hook or similar instrument to gently push out points and curves in designs. Stuff, and whipstitch the opening.

Thread a needle with a fairly long thread and knot the ends together. Slip the needle between whipstitches in the opening, and pull the knot into the ornament. Sew on the beads, bits of felt, and buttons to complete the design, going through stuffing from one bead or button to the next. Add a loop of gold thread for hanging.

PACKAGE TIES AND POCKET PETS

Tie a felt cookie onto a package or stuff one as a small gift for a child. Make the felt tie-on as described above, wrap the packages, tie a bow, and tack teddy bears or gingerbread men to the ends of the ribbon. (If you want to make teddy bears and cannot find a cutter, make a cardboard outline by modifying a gingerbread man—

just draw on some ears and shift the position of the hands.) For a child's party, make felt tie-ons as place-marker favors. Loop the ribbons around the backs of chairs, tie bows, and add cards with children's names.

Note: Beads and baubles are endlessly fascinating to children, but they may be inappropriate for very small tots! Eliminate the danger of swallowing buttons and beads by replacing them with French knots and a few satin stitches on teddy bears and gingerbread men. You can make a reindeer pocket pet that is safe for a young tot by making French-knot eyes and adding a few satin stitches to the saddle. Make a star shape in bright red, and a small child will never miss the beads.

Victorian Tree under Glass

A tiny tree, laden with miniatures, takes on more sparkle and an air of mystery when it is displayed beneath a glass dome. With the dome surrounding the tree, it seems to be set off in its own small world.

Since the glass dome is the most unusual item needed for this project, select your dome first. A dome about 14″ high is used in the tree shown here. Then select a cone that fits into the dome, being sure to allow for the layer of statice that will cover the tree on all sides.

MATERIALS:
 glass dome and base
 cone of plastic foam
 dried statice
 olive-green floral spray
 tiny tree trims
 white household glue (optional)

Select small pieces (about 1½″ long) of the dried statice and dip the ends in glue. Beginning at the base of the plastic foam, insert the pieces to

cover the entire surface of the cone; as you work, place the dome over the tree occasionally to be sure you are not making the statice covering so thick that the dome will no longer fit.

When the cone is completely covered, spray it with a green floral spray. After the paint has dried, attach the cone to the base of the dome with glue.

Decorate the tree with garlands of by-the-yard craft pearls, packages that are sugar cubes wrapped in gift wrap, tiny seals, and other small items. Keep in mind the proportions of the tree and use only the smallest of trims for the best results. Attach the trims with straight pins or small wires. Place the dome over the tree.

Organdy for Christmas?

Such sheer fabric in the middle of winter? In clear, sharp red and soft, delicate white, organdy can introduce a gentle counterpoint to the stronger textures of the season. A white organdy dove—enhanced by white embroidery and pearls—can be used as the focal point of a wreath, as the topper of a table decoration, or as a contrasting shape against the background of a green tree. Organdy baskets, shaped with glue over mundane spray-paint cans, zing with rich color to add charm to your party table.

ORGANDY BASKETS

For an elegant luncheon—or to delight a group of children—fashion organdy baskets to hold candies or other small favors. Organdy of 100% cotton works best for making the baskets, but a lining fabric or calico may also be used.

MATERIALS:
  fabric (each basket requires two
     6"-diameter circles)
  white household glue
  ribbon (11" for each basket)
  small silk flowers
  waxed paper
  masking tape
  tall spray-paint can or similarly shaped
     object to use as a form
  toothpicks

Press fabric and cut two 6"-diameter circles for each basket. Cover the tops of the spray cans with waxed paper and secure with masking tape. Cover work surfaces with newspaper since the glue will drip. Mix equal parts glue and water, preferably in a bowl near the size of the circles of organdy.

Dip a circle of fabric into the glue mixture until the fabric is saturated. Smooth fabric between fingers, pressing out as much glue as possible without wrinkling the fabric. Center the fabric circle on the top of the can. Arrange the edges into attractive fluted folds and allow to dry undisturbed. When the circle is thoroughly dry, drape a second glue-saturated circle over the first. Flute the edges so that wherever the first layer curves out, the second curves in to touch it and outward curves of the second layer are opposite inward curves of the first circle. Allow to dry completely. Dip an 11" piece of ribbon into the glue mixture and hang from one end to dry.

When the basket is dry, carefully remove it from the can, and separate the waxed paper from the fabric. Trim any raveled edges. Curve the ribbon into a handle and, with undiluted glue, secure the ends between layers of fabric.

Attach tiny silk flowers for a final delicate touch; with a toothpick, apply a dot of glue to the backs of the flowers and hold in place with straight pins until the glue dries.

EMBROIDERED DOVES

Doves in two sizes are delicately embroidered in cotton threads and pearly beads on white organdy and stuffed with soft fiberfill. Small doves are shown on the tree and perched on the cluster of cinnamon sticks. A larger dove adorns the wreath shown on page 34.

MATERIALS:
patterns on pages 138-139
⅓ yard white cotton organdy (will make 3 large or 5 small doves)
polyester fiberfill
white pearl cotton embroidery thread (large doves)
white cotton embroidery floss (small doves)
imitation seed pearls, 1 package each of tiny, medium, and medium-elongated
white sewing thread
1 yard (⅛"-wide) white satin ribbon

Place organdy over patterns for dove and wing. Transfer outline and embroidery details to fabric. Reverse the pattern and trace for back of bird and second wing.

Work embroidered design on all pieces with outline and lazy-daisy stitches. With smaller needle and sewing thread, sew pearls in place as indicated on the pattern: small dots for tiny

pearls, larger dots for medium pearls, and dark, elongated shapes for the elongated pearls. Press all pieces. Cut out pieces, leaving ½" margin of fabric around each piece.

Pin body front and back, right sides together, matching outlines. Sew by machine along outline, leaving open between "Xs" for turning. Trim seam allowance to 3/16". Clip curves, turn body right side out, and press.

Stuff lightly and whipstitch the opening.

Press wings. Trim along tracing line. Fold into fan shape along fold lines on pattern.

Baste wing into position on body. Using embroidery thread, work buttonhole stitches between markings to secure wing. Repeat for the other wing.

For the large dove, cut a 12" piece of ribbon and tie in a bow around dove's neck.

For the small dove, cut a 7" piece of ribbon. Tack center of ribbon to back of dove. Tie ends together in a bow at top of loop for hanging.

VINE WREATH WITH DOVE

Red cranberries, golden cord, and holly complement the white dove on a vine wreath.

MATERIALS:
 grapevines or other vines
 2 yards gold cord
 white household glue
 small package cranberries
 sewing thread
 fresh holly
 large dove

Make a vine wreath. (Instructions are given with Low Country Wreath, page 18.)

Loop gold cord loosely over the front of the wreath. Secure with a drop of glue in several places where the cord crosses vines.

Thread a needle with a length of sewing thread and knot the ends together. String the cranberries; tie short strings together into a longer string. Drape the cranberries over the vine wreath, and secure at several intervals with short pieces of wire or string.

Insert sprigs of fresh holly into the bottom third of the wreath. Perch the dove in place. Thread a needle with white thread and make loops through the bottom of the body at back and front to tie in place.

DOVES ON CINNAMON STICKS

A bright and puffy red print bow tops a cluster of cinnamon sticks to make a perfect perch for a small dove. Snips of pine add a contrasting touch of green. This arrangement can accent a side table or be used as a centerpiece.

Timeless & Simple
Add grace and charm to a room with this most traditional of decorations—but with the arrangement made unusually impressive by its generous proportions. Select a beautiful—and large—basket. Fill it with large pinecones, clusters of nandina berries, and fresh pine. Add a puffy plaid bow that is scaled to the size of the basket.

For a Collector Do you collect angels? Their delicate shapes and muted colors can be appreciated best at close range. A grouping of angels at each place will allow dinner guests to enjoy a collection. A crocheted tablecloth—a treasured family keepsake—is placed over another cloth of blue moiré to provide the setting for the angels, a centerpiece of roses and candles, and china and crystal with flower designs.

Reflections Light and color are multiplied in the mirror that provides a base for the centerpiece, in the facets of the candleholders, in the silver table appointments, and in the silver-wrapped gifts that top the stately but restrained china. The color is supplied by camellias—there are fewer than one might think—and by the red candles and napkins. Camellias at either side of the centerpiece rest on the mirror—the florist's vials that keep them fresh hidden with curls of graceful ribbon that are also multiplied by the mirror.

Fabulous Foils

The tree shown here is in a Victorian "little room" with furniture dating from 1867 and wallpaper with extravagant fringed borders. The tree is balsam, the traditional Victorian Christmas tree. Ornaments are a cheerful mixture of turn-of-the-century antiques and brand new foil ornaments and monograms.

The foil used to make these ornaments is 36-gauge aluminum craft foil. If you are unable to find this foil, make the ornaments from the bottoms of aluminum pie pans. If the foil has wrinkles or dents, remove them before you start the ornaments by placing the foil between two pieces of paper and smoothing it with a spoon.

MATERIALS:
   patterns on pages 138-139
   36-gauge aluminum craft foil (or aluminum pie pans)
   lacquer-based paints (the kind used for painting on glass)
   lacquer thinner
   several inexpensive paint brushes with fine points
   tracing paper
   thread or ornament hook

Trace the patterns onto tracing paper. In addition to the designs shown here, you can find inspiration for others by using Christmas cards or picture books of fish, birds, and flowers. Lots of surface texture strengthens the foil, so include as much as you can. For instance, the scales of a fish can cover the entire surface.

Place the tracing of the design over the foil and draw over the outlines with a pencil. Cut out around the outlines of the design with scissors. Then replace the tracing of the pattern on the foil, and draw with the pencil over the lines of the textured parts of the design. It is the pressure of the pencil that makes the texture of the design; experiment with different pressures and with using the tip of the pencil for dots. For deeper grooves, place the foil on several layers of newspaper—the softer the surface, the deeper the grooves.

Thin the lacquer paint with thinner to make it transparent. Paint the ornaments in the colors suggested in the photographs or in a wide variety of colors. To prevent runs when you use more than one color on an ornament, allow one painted area to dry before painting an adjacent area with a different color.

To hang the ornament, estimate the center of balance and push a straight pin through the foil. Thread with a piece of thread, or use a wire hanger through the hole.

GOLDEN MONOGRAMS

Tinsel initials, monograms, and even short names can be shaped from metallic chenille stems. Simply shape the chenille stems into the letters, and tie the letters together to form names. Personalize a tree by adding a monogram for each member of the family. Try these for name tags on gifts as well.

A Personal Vignette

A table skirt, overskirt, frames for favorite photographs, and even matching pillows coordinate with each other and with your room because you choose the fabrics and colors for your own style and taste. There are numerous wonderful holiday prints available—from country calicoes to formal stripes—and one is sure to be just right for a table skirt for your room. Add an easy-to-make overskirt with perky red bows. Group your favorite photographs into a Christmas gallery with frames and mats you make to fit the scene. Slipcover pillows in matching holiday prints. As a finishing touch, hang a festive kissing ball in a window.

TABLE SKIRT

MATERIALS:
fabric (see measuring instructions below)
matching thread

A table skirt such as the one shown in the photograph is nothing more than a large circle of cloth with a hem. To determine the size for your circle, you need to know the exact diameter of the table and the exact height from the *top* of the table to the floor. Add the diameter of your table plus *twice* the height of the table plus two inches for hem. For example, a table that is 26″ high and 30″ in diameter would require fabric that is 84″ long (30″ plus 52″ plus 2″).

The fabric must be a square, both as wide and as long as your measurement. When you know the length, determine how many widths of cloth will be necessary to make a square. Unless the table is very large, two widths of fabric will be adequate. For example, two widths of 45″ fabric with seams will be wide enough for a skirt that is 88″ in diameter; wider fabrics could be used for a larger table. Purchase material that is equal to the length you need (84″ in the example given) multiplied by the number of widths (probably 2).

To combine the widths to the right size, cut your fabric to the length of your measurement. A seam through the top and center of a cloth is very noticeable and distracting; therefore, cut one length of your fabric down the fold so that you have two narrow lengths. Matching any print, stripe, or plaid that you may be using, sew the half-width on either side of your full width. You now have a large piece of material with the seams where they will fall unnoticed at the sides of the skirt. (Figure 1.)

The resulting piece of fabric will be quite large. To make it easier to handle, fold it very carefully and evenly into fourths. You may want to stabilize the material on a cutting board with pins or thumbtacks. You must now mark a radius (half the measurement that you have so carefully established). One way to mark this radius is to pin a string *at center of the fabric* (corner where folds meet) and attach a piece of chalk at the other end, with the length of the string exactly the same as your radius. Use the chalk as a compass to draw the line. (Figure 2.) With a yardstick, double check by measuring at several intervals to determine that the distance from the center to the line is correct and consistent; the chalk can tip somewhat as you draw.

Cut the fabric, one layer at a time, using the chalk mark for the first layer and then using the cut edge as a guide for subsequent layers.

Once you have cut your full circle of material, you have practically finished. Turn under the edge ½″, then ½″ again, and hem on the machine with a running stitch.

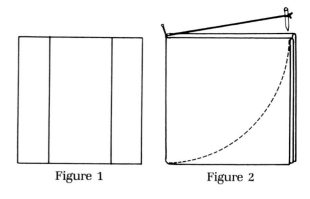

Figure 1   Figure 2

shown here is about 14″, but this could vary a few inches. (Try to plan overskirt so you use only one width of cloth; for the overskirt in the photograph, for example, a 30″-diameter top and 2 sides of 14″ were cut from 58″ materials. Check drapery departments of fabric stores for wide widths.) To the diameter of your table, add *twice* the depth of the drop and a hem allowance of 1″. This will give you the diameter of the circle that you will need to cut from the fabric. To cut your circle, follow the cutting instructions given with the table skirt.

Turn under ¼″, then ¼″ again, and hem with a running stitch.

To determine the placement of the six ribbon drawstrings, fold the skirt in half and mark the outside edges of the fold with pins. Leaving the skirt folded in half, fold in thirds (Figure 3) to find the placement for the other four ribbons. Mark with pins.

Place the skirt on the table, wrong side up. Stretch yarn or string from one of the pins to the pin on the opposite side of the table. Mark with pins the spots along this line that are just below the edge of the table. Mark the other lines in the same way. (Figure 4.) Run a basting line from pin at table edge to pin at outside edge. (Figure 5.)

Sew two channels of bias tape, one just on either side of the basting thread. Cut ribbon into 18″ lengths and run from outer edges through channels until ends of ribbons reach the point where the channels meet table edge. Sew across ribbons and channel ends at table edge.

Place the cloth on the table and draw the ribbons to gather the cloth along the channels. The ribbons can be released for laundering.

TABLE OVERSKIRT

MATERIALS:
  white fabric (see measuring instructions below)
  white thread
  6 yards white single-fold bias tape
  6 yards (⅜″ wide) red grosgrain ribbon

Measure the diameter of your table. Now decide how deep you will make the drop around the sides; the depth of the drop

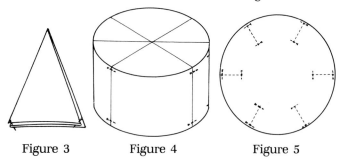

Figure 3   Figure 4   Figure 5

HOLIDAY FRAMES

Do you collect a favorite new photograph each Christmas? And do you have a group of favorites that you would like to display if only they were not such different sizes and shapes that you could never find frames and mats for all of them? Adapt a set of frames—collected from the attic, garage sales, or dimestore—to display Santa-shots and snapshots. After the holidays, the photographs can easily be slipped from the mounts and returned to the safety of their albums.

MATERIALS:
   frames
   red spray paint
   lightweight cardboard for mats
   fabric in a Christmas print for mats
   fusible bond
   photo mounts

Collect a group of frames. Sizes, shapes, age, and quality can vary since they will be painted. The smallest frame shown is a dimestore "gold" frame, and the largest is an old one found at a garage sale.

Remove the glass and backings from the frames. Spray paint the frames red, using several light coats to cover well.

Using lightweight cardboard, cut mats for each of the frames. Cut fabric and the fusible bond to the size of each of the mats. Following the manufacturer's directions, use fusible bond to attach the fabric to the cardboard.

Using photo mounts, position the photographs on the mats. Place glass, mats, and backings in frames.

SLIPCOVERS FOR PILLOWS

Slipcover pillows with the corners cut away from the table skirt or from an extra half yard of the fabric that is used for mats. Measure your pillow. Add 1" for seam allowances to each measurement. Cut 2 pieces of fabric to these measurements. Sew around fabric except for an opening along one side. Turn the cover, press, slip onto the pillow, and whipstitch together.

KISSING BALL

Steal a kiss from your Santa beneath the mistletoe. This kissing ball is made on a base of a potato, and will last for a surprisingly long time.

MATERIALS:
   large potato
   18" strong but flexible wire
   florist's picks with wires
   cedar
   1½ yards ribbon
   mistletoe

Choose a firm, large potato. Push a strong but flexible wire from top to bottom and back to top of potato. Twist the ends of the wire into a loop.

Gather sprigs of cedar into a cluster, and wire together with a florist's pick. Push the picks into the potato to form a full ball, covering the potato completely. Trim sprigs that are uneven, so the ball shape is maintained. Add a long loop of ribbon for hanging. Make a bow from the ribbon, and attach with a florist's pick. Finish the design with a sprig of mistletoe, wired to a florist's pick and pushed into place.

Apple Rings

Nothing could be simpler than to string rings of dried apples onto wire—and that is exactly how these small "country" kitchen wreaths are made. Their soft colors and pleasing apple aroma will add just the right touch to a kitchen or family room. Each wreath requires two (6-ounce) packages of dried apple rings, 15" of wire, and ribbon for a bow and hanger. Slip the rings onto the wire, bend into a circle, and fasten the ends of the wire together. Attach a bow.

Capture a Snowflake

Grownups who enjoyed making paper chains and cutting snowflake silhouettes as children can graduate happily to constructing this three-dimensional paper decoration. The materials are nothing more than white paper and glue. The full-sized pattern is ready for tracing.

MATERIALS:
   pattern on page 137
   typing paper or similar white paper
   white household glue
   8" string
   small strip white cardboard
   white ribbon for hanging
   red satin ribbon for bow
   holiday greenery

Trace the pattern onto the white paper. Place the tracing over three more sheets of paper. Using a craft knife, cut through all thicknesses. Repeat to make a total of 12 pieces. With a hole punch, make holes at base (circles on pattern).

Divide the paper pieces into pairs, and glue the pieces of each pair along the center line of the pattern. Allow to dry thoroughly.

Glue the pairs together at the points of the pattern marked by "X," joining the pairs in a stack of all the pieces.

Place the string through the two sets of holes at the base of the pattern, and tie very loosely so that the pieces can move freely.

Cut two strips of cardboard 5½" × ⅜". Glue these to the center line of the top and bottom pieces along the center line of the pattern. Allow to dry.

Pull the cardboard strips together to guide the snowflake into its circular shape. A bit of tape, rolled with the sticky side out, will hold the cardboard strips together and can be removed after the holidays. If the tape is removed and the snowflake folded together, it can be saved and used another year.

Glue a length of narrow ribbon to suspend the snowflake in the window. Add sprigs of greenery and a bow of the satin ribbon to complete the decoration.

Quiet Tones

In a striking blend of dried materials and shiny evergreens, this mantel arrangement combines a wide variety of textures and color tones. Dried materials include hydrangeas, eucalyptus, popcorn plant, pinecones, and the limbs from corkscrew willow. Pine, nandina berries, and waxy magnolia are the fresh accents.

Easy Accents

Brass candlesticks, metallic gold ribbon, burnished copper, and plenty of candlelight add seasonal brilliance to this shelf. The arrangement is just as festive as any red-and-green decoration could be, yet it complements its surroundings.

A Touch of Glitter

Gold metallic ribbon—nothing more—changes a vine wreath from simple to luxurious. (For instructions on making a vine wreath, see Low Country Wreath, page 18.) A collection of brass candlesticks repeats the metallic sheen of the ribbon, and the flickering light of the candles sets the scene aglow.

A pineapple rests proudly atop a pyramid of apples in the historic Hammond-Harwood House in Annapolis.

A pyramid of holly, boxwood, lemons, and berries is used in the Robert Mills House in Columbia, South Carolina. Since the house was built for an Englishman before Christmas trees were introduced in this country, the festivities lean toward wassail and plum pudding—and pyramids.

Fruit Pyramids

The fruit pyramid was one of the most popular decorations in colonial America. It was brought by settlers from England where it had long been a seasonal favorite. In America, it acquired the pineapple that has become a customary topper. The most common pyramids of eighteenth-century America used a combination of apples and a pineapple. Some thrifty cooks, torn between decoration and Christmas dinner, used only the top of the pineapple. This happened so often that the custom acquired a name; if only the top of the pineapple is used, the pyramid is topped with a "deceit."

Although most records mention apples and pineapples, it is likely that a much wider variety of fruits was used. Our ancestors seem to have adapted many basic ideas—such as the English pyramid—to fit the circumstances of their lives in a new land.

BASES FOR PYRAMIDS

Colonial women often built their pyramids upon a base of three cabbages in graduated sizes. The largest cabbage was sliced to provide a level base on a platter. Then a medium-sized and a small cabbage were stacked on the large cabbage. Knitting needles pushed through cabbages from top to bottom held the base together. (Barbeque skewers work as well.) To support a pineapple, the top was also sliced to provide a level surface.

Wooden cones with spikes soon became popular. They can be used for years and are sometimes available through museum and specialty shops.

Another base can be adapted from a readily available material of this century just as the colonial woman adapted her cabbages; a cone of plastic foam with a flattened top is perhaps the easiest base to use.

TO MAKE A PYRAMID

Select a base, and place it on a large platter.

Select the fruit, and if you are using a wooden cone, impale the fruit on the spikes. If you are

Lemons and whitespot Japanese pittosporum are used in this pyramid from the Magevney House, the oldest standing residence in Memphis.

using a cabbage base or a cone of plastic foam, attach the fruit onto florist's picks as described on page 23. (The green dye used in some florist's picks is poisonous; do not eat fruit that has been punctured by the picks.) Use an ice pick or skewer to punch holes in the base. Beginning at the bottom, insert picks in the holes. To set a pineapple or a deceit at the top of the pyramid, make three holes in the top. Push the blunt ends of florist's picks into the holes, and push the pineapple onto the sharp ends of the picks.

Starting at the bottom, push sprigs of boxwood, holly, or other greenery between the fruit. Crowd the greenery enough to hold it in place.

In the Magevney House, a fruit pyramid is at the center of a table arrangement of fruit and greenery. A wreath at the window also boasts fruit as a decoration.

47

Under the Tree
This array of toys began as an alternative to wrapping and displaying gifts beneath the tree. Santa brought most of the gifts in this family, and few gifts remained under the tree throughout the season. So the tree would not seem bare, toys from other years were set beneath the tree. The collection has grown through the years, and now, with children in college, the toys remain a traditional part of the family celebration.

Moss Wreath & Heart

Velvety-soft moss is shaped into wreaths and hearts and accented with straw flowers and ribbons. Dried sheet moss is used in the wreath and heart shown here, but experiment with Spanish moss and other mosses to discover the designs that you can create for yourself.

MOSS WREATH

MATERIALS:
   12″ diameter straw wreath
   18″ wire
   thick glue
   dried sheet moss
   1 yard (1″-wide) ribbon
   dried straw flowers
   dried yarrow

Wrap 12″ length of wire around the straw wreath, and twist together to form a loop.

Cover the straw wreath with the thick glue, and push the moss firmly into the glue. When the front of the wreath is firmly covered, turn the wreath and cover the back.

Tie the ribbon into a bow, leaving 8″ streamers. Place a 6″ wire through the back of the bow and push the wire into the wreath. Add dried straw flowers with glue if they do not have wire stems; if the flowers do have wire stems, push the stems into the wreath. Place the streamers in a pleasing position, and glue the streamers to the moss. Attach small pieces of dried yarrow with glue.

MOSS HEART

Instead of a traditional wreath for your Christmas decorating, this year make a heart to hang on a mirror or above a mantel. The moss heart is made in the same manner as the moss wreath, except that the base is made of plastic foam. Either purchase a heart-shaped piece of plastic foam or cut a heart shape from a block.

Subtle Shades of Autumn

The rich textures and subtle colors of this wreath convey the sophistication that comes only from absolute simplicity. Savor the memory of an autumn afternoon in wide open fields as you combine rabbit tobacco and red peppers into this wreath that will last through winter. As the vivid colors of summer give way to the delicate shades and seedpods of autumn, gather rabbit tobacco from the fields and hang by the stems to dry. At the same time, air dry spicy, pungent peppers from the garden. When the rabbit tobacco is dry, spray it with a fixative or with hair spray; the peppers need no special treatment.

MATERIALS:
    straw wreath form
    enough rabbit tobacco to cover wreath
        form completely
    about 70 red peppers
    florist's picks with wires
    wire for hanger

Cut rabbit tobacco into small pieces. Gather the pieces into clusters, and wrap each cluster with the wire of a florist's pick. Cover the wreath form completely with the tobacco, working in the same direction around the wreath so that each additional cluster conceals the stem ends and pick of the previous cluster. Wire the peppers in groups of three to florist's picks. Space the peppers around the wreath. Wrap wire around the wreath form and form a loop for hanging.

Cones & Such

Scrub pine, Norway spruce, Colorado spruce pine, Australian pine, sweet gum, oak. The hard seed cases from these trees, with their fascinating shapes and intricate designs, can be the bases for ornaments that Mother Nature never even considered. Just go for a walk in the woods and gather as many varieties of cones and seed cases as you can find. The instructions below will tell you which cones were used in the ornaments shown here, but you can look at the photographs and select a cone that is similar in size and shape.

In December, the Southern Highland Handicraft Guild holds a "Christmas with the Guild" at the Folk Art Center near Asheville, North Carolina. This event—which actually lasts through most of the month and features a number of individual programs—includes theme trees, musical programs, an international tree-trimming party and programs for children. A favorite feature each year is the Members' Tree which displays hundreds of ornaments handcrafted by the members of the Guild.

As a part of the "Christmas with the Guild" program, a dozen or more theme trees are trimmed by several garden clubs in the area who choose themes on the bases of local culture, state symbols, legends, etc. Winning trees are chosen. The tree that won first place in 1982 was designed by the Haw Creek Garden Club. The theme of that tree was "Pinecones and Native Materials," and some of their ornaments are shown here.

CONE FLOWERS

Cone flowers can be made with a variety of small cones. The flowers will change their character with a change of cones, but each will have its own fragile beauty.

Cover wire with florist's tape, and wrap the wire around the lower part of a cone. Pull the wire tightly together and down to the base of the cone. This wire will form the stem and be used for wiring the flower onto the branch of the tree.

Just above the line of wire around the cone, begin to arrange petals of lunaria (money plant), slipping the petals into the cone. Place each petal in front of the petal before it, overlapping approximately half the first petal. Repeat around the cone, adding petals until you are pleased with the arrangement. The last petal should be placed in front of the other petals, but the last side should be tucked behind another petal. Wire the flower to the branch of the tree.

ANGEL

To the base of a cone from a scrub pine, glue two acorn caps for feet. Glue an acorn with a cap at the top of the cone for a head. Cut a double wing shape from stiff burlap and glue to cone. Cut a rectangle for a book, and slip into the cone. Wrap wire near the base, pulling it tightly into the cone so it does not show from the front, and wire the angel to the tree.

CANDLE

Dip a pipe cleaner in orange paint. Cut the base of a cone from a Norway spruce. Glue a Colorado spruce pine cone on top of the base of the other cone. Glue on a flame that is a ½"-long snip from the pipe cleaner. Wire the base of the candle, and attach to tree with the wire.

WREATH

For the wreath, simply select seven sweet gum balls, drill holes through them, and string onto 24-gauge wire. Twist into a circle, glue on straw-flowers, and add a bow.

POODLES

Select eleven Australian pine cones and glue them together with tacky glue as shown in the photograph: 1 head with 1 nose and 2 ears, 2 cones for the body, 4 legs and the tail.

Cranberry Candle Ring

Surround a candle and its hurricane shade with a ring of cranberries to make this festive center-piece. The cranberries will last about a week when they are dipped in liquid floor wax to preserve them. (You will need to tell children *not* to taste.)

MATERIALS:
 2 to 3 packages fresh cranberries
 clear liquid floor wax
 platter
 wreath form of plastic foam
 green foil
 long straight pins
 cedar or other greenery
 ribbon for bow
 2 florist's picks

Dip the cranberries in the clear floor wax and allow them to dry overnight on newspaper.

Select a platter or other round dish that is a little larger than the wreath form. The platter is necessary because the cranberries will stain. Adapt a platter that is incompatible in color by wrapping it in green foil.

Wrap the wreath form in green foil. Push the long straight pins through the cranberries and into the wreath form.

Wire sprigs of greenery to a florist's pick and push the pick into the wreath. Make a bow of the ribbon, wire it to a florist's pick, and attach it to the wreath.

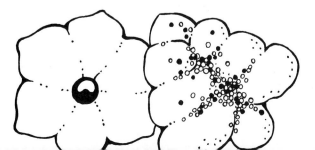

Cookie Candleholders

Make these party decorations from cookie dough that you pick up from the refrigerator case in the supermarket. We used the peanut-butter flavored dough, and the whole room smelled great for days.

MATERIALS:
   patterns on page 135
   lightweight cardboard for patterns
   one package (12 ounces) cookie dough
      for each candleholder
   a clean bottle cap with a diameter
      slightly larger than the diameter of
      your candles
   a small plate for each candleholder
   candles

Trace the 3 star patterns. Place the tracing over lightweight cardboard and cut through tracing and cardboard to make a pattern.

Using a cookie sheet with a non-stick surface or a liner of foil, roll out the dough to ¼" thickness on the cookie sheet.

Place the large star pattern on the dough and mark around it with a knife. Remove the pattern, and cut away the dough that surrounds the star. Prepare the two smaller stars on a second cookie sheet, leaving at least 2" between cookies.

Cook as directed by dough manufacturer, but watch the timing carefully. Because the cookies are so large they will probably need an additional 2 to 3 minutes to brown.

Remove the cookies from the oven. Immediately make a hole in the center of each large cookie by using the bottle cap as a cutter. Allow the cookies to cool *on the pan*.

Using melted wax, stand the candle in the center of your dish. Slide the cookies, biggest first, over the candle.

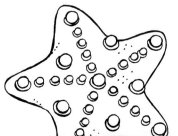

Christmas Bazaar

ome gifts must be special—because they are for special people—and Christmas decorations need a personal, handcrafted touch. The gifts and decorations on the following pages are special because you make them yourself. If you like to sew, to crochet, to needlepoint, to cross-stitch, to work with wood, to cut and glue—you will find new ways to use your talents in the ideas in this chapter.

You will find stockings, ornaments, wreaths, a choir for your mantel, a teddy for a gift or for decorating a table, a handsome sailor jumping jack, a Christmas picture to embroider, a card basket, sachets, and more. For each design, there are complete instructions, and any patterns you need can be found in the back of the book—full size and ready to use.

Children approach Christmas with boundless energy and enthusiasm, and a Children's Workshop is filled with answers to their questions of, "What can I do now?" There are bulletin boards and bookmarks to make for friends and family and folded baskets and shiny star baskets to hang on the tree. With a Christmas twirler, children can pop Santa into his sleigh and watch the reindeer run.

Wrap gifts in papers, bags, baskets, and boxes that carry your personal stamp. Easy touches turn ordinary muslin into reindeer bags and market baskets into bath accessories.

You will enjoy using your talents to craft gifts and decorations, and the people you love will treasure their gifts—because you made something just for them.

Easy Holiday Crafts

A Choir of Friendly Folk

These warm and friendly folk look as though they have just stepped from someone's Christmas dream of Old World carolers. Let the chubby-cheeked sock dolls with bean-bag bodies gather for an evening of holiday caroling on your mantel or table. A look at the patterns will convince you that they are not hard to make; changing fabrics in clothing accounts for the variety in appearances.

MATERIALS:

> pattern on pages 140-141
> child's nylon ankle socks
> polyester stuffing
> muslin or other solid-colored fabric
>   for body
> dried beans
> remnants of fabric for clothing
> buttons and trims
> embroidery floss for eyes
> pink felt for nose and ears
> bits of yarn for hair

To make the head, cut along the back side of sock so it will open flat. Trace pattern for head, pin to sock, and cut. Run gathering thread around outside of circle and gather slightly. Insert stuffing into circle, and continue gathering to close. Secure with several stitches. To make the eyes, sew several parallel stitches with embroidery floss, making each stitch about ⅛" long and sewing completely through the head to give form to the face. To make the mouth, sew stitches to outline a circle for a mouth opening, using sewing thread and stitching completely through the head. Cut nose and ears from felt, and sew or glue in place.

For the body, trace the pattern and cut 2 bodies and 1 base from muslin or any solid fabric. With right sides together, sew side seams of body. Pin base to body, right sides together, and sew. Turn. Fill body half full with dried beans. Continue filling body with stuffing. Pleat the side seams at the neck opening to form a smaller opening. Whipstitch together.

The clothing, whether it is the dress for the girl or the coat for the boy, is cut by the same pattern; the major difference is that the dress closes in the back while the coat overlaps in the front. Trace coat and sleeve patterns. Cut 1 coat and 2 sleeves for each caroler. Fold sleeves, right sides together, and sew underarm seam. Turn and press. Make hands by cutting two 1" squares from sock. Place a small amount of stuffing in center. Pull sock over stuffing and sew. Turn under ¼" on end of sleeve. Insert hand into sleeve, and sew sleeve together to secure hand. Repeat for other hand and arm. Fold coat or dress, right sides together, along arm openings. Pin the sleeves in the arm openings on the dress or the coat. Sew along the seamline. Turn under ¼" along the bottom edge of garment and hem by machine.

For the girl's dress, fold right sides together and sew back of dress. Cut cape from remnant; turn under ¼" hem all around and sew. Add trim.

For the boy's coat, turn under ¼" on long edges and stitch. Overlap edges for front of coat and secure with buttons. Cut cap from remnant, using the pattern for the base to cut the circle. Sew brim with right sides together. Turn and press. Turn under edges of circle and gather slightly. Sew brim to gathered circle.

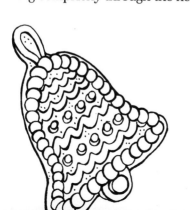

54

Slip the body into the coat or dress. Fold in side seams at neck edge to fit. Sew together along neck. For girls, attach cape in same way.

Position the head over the neck extension and sew in place. Cover neck and back of head with cap or scarf (a triangle of fabric). Sew securely in place. Add loops of yarn for hair and scarves for boys. Cut books from old Christmas cards or gift boxes. Tack loosely to inside of hands.

Grandmother's Special

Share a project with a grandchild or favorite niece. After a child paints a picture on fabric (using the fabric paints that are so easy to find now in fabric stores and craft shops), a grown-up adds a ruffle and backing to turn the painting into a pillow for the child's room. This is an excellent project to paint during the Thanksgiving holidays and finish in time to return for Christmas.

Mounting fabric on cardboard makes an instant and portable work surface. One advantage with the fabric paints is that they are opaque. If a "mistake" is made in painting, allow the fabric and paint to dry completely. Then paint over the problem.

MATERIALS:
2 (16") squares of white fabric
fabric for ruffle (90" long, 5" wide)
cardboard for mounting
masking tape
fabric paints
paintbrush
piping (optional)
white thread
90" ribbon for ruffle trim
polyester stuffing

Mount one 16" square of the white fabric on a piece of cardboard with masking tape to make it easier to handle.

Have the child paint a picture with the fabric paints. Allow the paint to dry thoroughly, and follow manufacturer's instructions for setting the paint.

To finish the pillow, Grandmother, cut a ruffle 5" wide and about 90" long. The ruffle shown here is of white fabric with ribbon at the edge, but a ruffle of print or colored fabric may be more suitable to frame your child's picture. Sew the ends of the ruffle, right sides together. Fold the ruffle, wrong sides together and lengthwise, and run a gathering thread ½" from the raw edges. Place ribbon at outside of ruffle, and sew along both edges of ribbon. Sew piping around edges of pillow front. Gather ruffle to fit the pillow front. With ruffle toward inside of pillow, match gathered edge to outside edge of pillow front. Pin; then sew.

Place back and front with right sides together, and sew again along seam line, leaving an opening for turning. Stuff the pillow, and whipstitch closed.

A Glint of Gold

Metallic canvas is a newcomer to the needle-point market. It has the virtues of plastic canvas because it can be cut to shape and will not ravel. It is, however, more pliable than regular plastic canvas and its metallic finish can be allowed to show through for highlights in your work. These pretty fans, baskets, and bells have different patterns on each side.

MATERIALS:
>   **charts and color key on pages 145-146**
>   **gold metallic needlepoint canvas (one**
>   **10″ × 12″ piece for 3 ornaments)**
>   **gold and silver metallic needlepoint yarn**
>   **tapestry wool in red, dark green, light**
>   **green, gold, ecru, black**
>   **#18 tapestry needle**
>   **scraps of red felt**
>   **scrap of lace**
>   **narrow red satin ribbon**

Work the designs according to the charts, using half-cross stitch throughout. Carefully cut out all the pieces, leaving one thread of canvas outside the stitched outline.

Assemble by whipping the pieces together with gold metallic yarn over the outer threads of the canvas. (The bell and basket have side pieces that are to be whipped between the front and back pieces.) For the fan, sew gathered lace to one side of long edge of fan, and close with sewing thread, as inconspicuously as possible. Whip the remaining sides of the fan directly together.

For the basket, cut a handle that is three threads wide and 6″ long. Whip along both sides with gold yarn and tack to basket. Cut an oval of red felt about 2″ × 5″, and tuck into basket.

Add tiny bows of red satin ribbon at sides of basket, tip of fan, and top of bell. Make loops for hanging from gold metallic yarn.

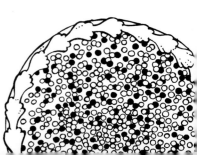

Christmas Greetings

Each Christmas, so many people send warm and friendly greetings in the form of Christmas cards. In the hustle and bustle of the season, however, we sometimes fail to take the time to enjoy and appreciate the cards. This basket is designed just to hold Christmas cards. And, if the basket itself is kept on the dinner table, you will find it easy to share the cards that arrive each day. Passing the new cards around the table will give you a chance to explain to the children just who Great Aunt Martha is and to reminisce about the good times you had with the Millers when they lived down the street.

MATERIALS:
    chart and color key on page 142
    basket, 5″ × 9″ (4″ deep)
    44″ × 6″ strip of #14 Aida cloth
    embroidery floss in red, green, and
      yellow
    2 yards (⅝″-wide) red grosgrain ribbon
    2 yards (⅜″-wide) red grosgrain ribbon
    about 28″ (¼″-wide) elastic

Turn under ⅝″ along one long side of the Aida cloth. Press. On the right side, place the ⅝″-wide ribbon along the edge, and topstitch along both sides of the ribbon, catching the turned-under Aida cloth as you sew.

Turn under 1″ along the other long side of the fabric. Press. On the right side, place the narrow ribbon ½″ from the edge. Sew along both sides of the ribbon, sewing through both thicknesses of the Aida cloth.

Work the tree design on the Aida with 3 strands of embroidery floss, centering the trees between the ribbons and spacing three intersections between the long bottom limbs of the trees as you repeat the design.

Cut elastic to fit around your basket, and run elastic through casing that is beneath the narrow red ribbon. Sew the ends of the strip together, catching the elastic as you sew. Slip the skirt onto the basket, and wrap the remaining ribbon around the handle of the basket.

Crocheted Angels

Make a delicate angel stocking with a panel of filet crochet atop luxurious, soft velvet. Another angel panel sewn to a cover of unbleached muslin will transform a blank book into a treasured Christmas diary (page 62).

FILET CROCHET

MATERIALS:
> diagram on page 61
> 1 ball ecru Knit-Cro-Sheen® cotton
>   crochet thread
> steel crochet hook, size 10

TERMS: ch (chain), st (stitch), sk (skip), dc (double crochet), sp (space), sc (single crochet), sl st (slip stitch), trc (triple crochet)

These instructions are for both the 4-angel panel for the stocking and for the single panel for the book.

Follow the instructions in regular type for both the stocking and the book. Add instructions in **darker** type for the stocking only. Add instructions in *italics* for book only.

Filet Crochet Border:
Ch 224 for stocking. *Ch 60 for book.*
Row 1: dc in 5th ch from hook, (ch 1, sk 1 ch, dc in next ch), across. **108 spaces for stocking;** *only 27 spaces for book.* Ch 4, turn.
Row 2: (dc in dc, ch 1), across, dc in 3rd ch of turning ch, two rows of mesh formed. Ch 4, turn.
Row 3: * (dc in dc, ch 1) 8 times, dc in dc, (dc in ch 1 sp, dc in dc) block made, repeat 9 times, (ch 1, dc in dc) 8 times, ch 1, dc in 3rd ch of ch 4, **ch 1, repeat from * 3 more times to end for stocking only.** Ch 4, turn.
Row 4: Refer to 4th row on chart, counting mesh and blocks as indicated. **Repeat row 4 four times to end.** Ch 4, turn.
Row 5-29: Follow chart. Do not break off at end. Ch 2, turn.

Top Edging:
Row 1: (sc in sp, sc in dc) **repeat across for stocking;** *repeat around panel for book.*
Row 2: * ch 7, sl st in 4th ch from hook, picot made, ch 3, sk 3 sc, sc in next sc, repeat from * **across for stocking;** *repeat all around for book.* Break off.

Bottom Edging for Stocking:
Tie on thread in corner st of filet row 1.
Row 1: ch 5, (trc in dc, ch 1) across, ch 2, turn.
Row 2: (sc in sp, sc in trc) across.
Row 3: * ch 7, sl st in 4th ch from hook, picot made, ch 3, sk 3 sc, sc in next sc, repeat from * across. Break off. Press crochet.

CROCHET & VELVET STOCKING

A grown-up lady or a little girl will find this oversized stocking equally suitable. Its ageless design combines a panel of four angels, two shades of velvet, feather stitching around heel and toe, and a flourish of satin ribbons.

Crochet a panel of four angels following the instructions and making changes as indicated in **darker** type.

MATERIALS:
panel of 4 angels
stocking pattern on pages 142-143
⅓ **yard ecru velvet**
¼ **yard medium brown velvet**
½ **yard ecru satin lining fabric**
⅔ **yard (⅛"-wide) medium brown satin ribbon**
⅔ **yard (⅛"-wide) dark brown satin ribbon**
⅔ **yard (⅜"-wide) medium brown satin ribbon**
8" (⅝"-wide) medium brown satin ribbon

Cut stocking pieces as indicated on pattern. Cut two top bands of medium brown velvet that measure 11½" x 7". Baste heel and toe patches in position. With right sides together, sew top bands to stocking front and back. Grade seam, and press.

Using the front of the stocking (stocking front and band sewn together) as a pattern, cut 2 pieces of satin for lining. Sew lining with right sides together. Trim seam, and clip curves. Pin stocking front and back with right sides together.

Sew, leaving top edge open. Trim seam, clip curves, turn, and press. Slip lining into stocking, wrong sides together. Fold top edges under 1" for stocking and slightly more for lining. Pin in place, and sew with a blind stitch.

Using crochet thread, feather stitch around heel and toe patches. Join filet crochet border at sides to form a circle, stitching by hand with crochet thread. Pin border to stocking, having edging and one row of mesh extending above edge of stocking and matching the seam in filet with back seam of stocking. Sew border by hand to stocking along top edge only.

Weave ⅛" medium brown ribbon through top mesh row. Bring ends of ribbon to inside and tie to secure. Weave ⅛" dark brown ribbon through bottom dc row. Tie. Weave ⅜" medium brown ribbon through bottom trc mesh row. Tie as before. Fold an 8" piece of (⅝"-wide) medium brown ribbon in half. Sew in place at back seam for hanger.

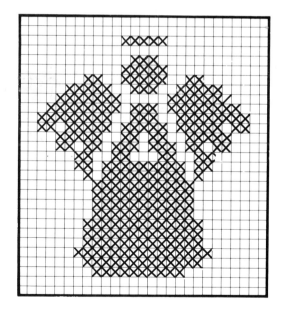

CHRISTMAS DIARY

Record happy memories of Christmas in this diary that is kept only once a year—but year after year. Five years from now, when you are trying to remember just who did come to dinner in 1983, you will be able to check the diary and bring back the pleasures of this holiday past. And this book is the perfect place to keep those addresses and phone numbers for the people you always contact at Christmas. Make diaries as gifts, and friends will cherish the gift and its thoughtful giver for years to come.

MATERIALS:
  one angel panel (instructions and chart
    on pages 60-61)
  blank book, 6¼" × 7½" or similar in size
  ⅓ yard unbleached muslin
  ⅓ yard medium-weight interfacing
  white sewing thread

Crochet one panel (beginning with a chain of 60, and making pattern changes as indicated in *italics*).

Blank books can come in a number of sizes, and the crocheted panel can also vary slightly in size. It is a good idea to take your finished angel panel to the store and "try on" books to find one that fits. The book should be a little larger than the crocheted angel panel.

Measure the height of your book and add 1" for seam allowances plus ½" for ease in slipping cover onto book. Measure the width of your book and the thickness of the spine of your book. Multiply the width by four; add one thickness of the spine and 1" for seam allowances plus ½" for ease. Cut a piece of muslin and a piece of interfacing to these two measurements. Place the interfacing on the wrong side of the fabric. Along the short sides, turn under ¼", then ¼" again, and sew in place for a hem. Fold the cover, right

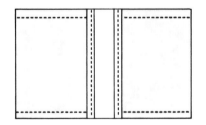

sides together, as shown in the diagram, making certain that the width of the cover is equal to the width of your book across front and back and including a spine thickness. Sew at top and bottom of cover, taking ½" seams. Turn and press. Slip the cover onto the book.

Place the crocheted panel on the book, and sew around all edges by hand.

62

Holiday Sachets

Potpourri-filled sachets can be used so many ways—as small gifts themselves, lagniappe for the outside of another present, favors for a party, or ornaments among the branches of your Christmas tree.

MATERIALS:

For print bag:
6″ × 6½″ scrap of cotton-blend print fabric
3″ × 6½″ scrap of coordinating fabric
2″ × 6½″ scrap of coordinating fabric
6½″ piece of eyelet
12″ ribbon
small flowers, pinecones, or leaves
potpourri
small piece of wire

For velvet bag:
6½″ × 6″ scrap of velvet
6½″ piece of narrow lace
6½″ piece of wide lace
12″ ribbon
small flowers, pinecones, or leaves
potpourri
small piece of wire

For the print bag: Along the 6½″ side of the largest piece of print fabric, place the 2″-wide strip of coordinating fabric with the right side facing the wrong side of the larger piece. Sew with a ½″ seam. Turn the seam and narrow strip to the top. Fold down the narrow strip ½″, then ½″ again, and topstitch.

Machine baste the eyelet across the 6½″ width of the bag, placing it 2½″ from the bottom. Fold down ½″ along the length of the remaining strip of coordinating fabric. Place over the edge of the eyelet and topstitch.

For the velvet bag: Hem top edge of velvet (along the 6½″ side). Topstitch the narrow lace along the top. Place the wide lace along the bottom of the bag. Stitch in place along the sides and bottom.

To complete both bags: Fold in half, right sides together. Stitch along the side and bottom, again using ½″ seams. Clip corners and turn.

Fill bag two-thirds full with potpourri. With wire, wrap small flowers, leaves, or cones around bag. Tie a ribbon over wire.

In a Nutshell

Make fruit and nut baskets from walnut halves, and fill with tiny artificial fruits and real cones. Make these as favors for a group, or hang them from the tree. Collect a number of small treasures to fill the baskets so that each will have its own character.

MATERIALS:
  walnut halves
  small amount of reeds or vines
  white household glue
  dried moss
  small bunches artificial fruit, small cones, grasses, yarn, etc.

Soak the reeds or vines for the handle in water until they are soft and pliable. Twist two reeds together, and glue ends inside opposite ends of the walnut. Allow the glue to dry, and partially fill the basket with moss. Finish filling with an assortment of dried cones, grasses, and pods combined with small artificial fruits and berries. Yarn can be tied into a bow of just the right size.

I Love My Teddy

Is there anyone who doesn't love a teddy bear? This sweet bear can sit on your mantel or on a table in an entryway to greet all your guests. Or, given a chance, he will entrance a child with bear secrets. He is 16½″ high and made from only three pattern pieces.

MATERIALS:
  pattern on pages 136-137
  1″ × 12″ × 24″ pine shelving
  latex gloss enamel paint in tan, brown, black, white, red, green, and yellow
  semigloss spray varnish
  6″ (½″-diameter) wooden dowel

Transfer pattern to wood. Cut around the outlines, using a jigsaw or band saw. Mark the dowel positions as shown on the patterns. Drill ½″ holes for the dowels. Sand all the edges and surfaces.

Transfer features for painting onto wood. Spray a thin coat of varnish over all surfaces and allow to dry completely. This will seal the wood and provide a better surface for painting. Paint the features as indicated on the pattern pieces. Dry overnight. Spray with a second coat of the varnish.

Cut the dowel into 2 (3″-long) pieces. Slide one dowel into the hole on one leg until the end of the dowel is flush with the outside leg surface. Slide the dowel through the hole in the body, and position the other leg onto the protruding portion of the dowel. All the dowels should fit tightly to allow for more controlled movement of the bear; there should be just a bit of space between the legs and body to prevent friction as the legs are moved. Attach arms, using the same method as for the legs.

Small Wreaths for the Tree

Make any or all of these small wreaths to hang as ornaments on your tree. From nature's bounty come the materials for the tiny vine wreaths, and wooden curtain rings form the bases for three quite different ornaments.

JUTE WREATH

MATERIALS:
  **2½″ diameter wooden curtain ring
    with hook
  60″ (5-ply) jute twine
  1 yard (¼″-wide) brown velvet ribbon
  small red berries, cones or acorns,
    sprigs of statice, licopodium
  hot glue or household cement**

Wrap ring with jute, and glue ends of jute. Arrange a bow made from velvet ribbon, decorative cones, and flowers at the top of the wreath. Attach with hot glue or household cement.

WREATH WITH GIFT PACKAGES

MATERIALS:
  **2½″ diameter wooden curtain ring
    with hook
  red latex paint
  small pieces of plastic foam
  gift paper in 5 different colors and
    patterns
  silver cord
  1 yard (¼″-wide) velvet ribbon
  hot glue or household cement**

Paint the curtain ring with the red latex paint. Cut the plastic foam to very small pieces, varying the sizes and shapes. (Measurements of pieces should vary from ¾″ to 1″.) Wrap in gift paper, and tie with cord. Glue packages to ring. Make a bow from velvet ribbon and glue at top of ring.

RIBBON-WRAPPED WREATH

MATERIALS:
  **2½″ diameter wooden curtain ring
    with hook
  red latex paint
  15 inches (½″-wide) embroidered trim
  1 yard (¼″-wide) velvet ribbon
  small bell
  hot glue or household cement**

Paint the curtain ring with the red latex paint. Wrap trim as shown in photograph; glue ends of trim in place on ring. Make bow from the velvet ribbon, and glue at the top of the wreath. Glue on the bell.

SMALL VINE WREATHS

Loop grapevine or other vine into a small wreath shape, weaving the ends of the vine to secure. Add narrow satin ribbons; one wreath shown here is looped with ribbon while the other has only a bow. Tuck in treasures from nature: a lichen-covered twig, Spanish moss, popcorn plant. Use any of the natural materials that are available to you in your area. To go with the wreaths, perch a small purchased red bird on a pinecone; wrap the cone with a wire and pull the wire beneath a branch to hold the cone and bird in place.

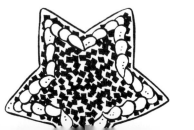

67

Sailor Jumping Jack

Jumping jacks have been favorite toys for centuries—and this new design is sure to win the heart of some little boy or girl. Jumping jacks were made in ancient Egypt and Greece. In eighteenth-century France, members of the royal circle vied with each other to assemble the biggest and best collection. This handsome sailor can be strung in the traditional way and hung as an ornament on your tree. But if the sailor is to find a permanent home on a child's wall, he can be mounted on a plaque.

MATERIALS:

> **pattern on page 143**
> **light wood (3/16" thick) with a low grain**
>   **pattern (bass or buckeye)**
> **fine sandpaper**
> **⅛"-diameter dowel**
> **drill and bits in ⅛", 3/16" and 1/32" sizes**
> **acrylic paints**
> **buttonhole twist or other heavy thread**
> **button or bead**
> **wooden plaque (about 4" × 7")**

Transfer pattern to wood. Cut out all pieces with a jigsaw. Place front and back pieces together and line up edges. Drill through both front and back to make holes at each of the four *large* dots on the pattern front, using a ⅛" drill bit. Using a 3/16" drill bit, drill a hole in each arm and leg at the *larger* dots. With a 1/16" drill bit, drill another hole in each arm and leg to make holes for string at the *small* dots. If you prefer *not* to mount the

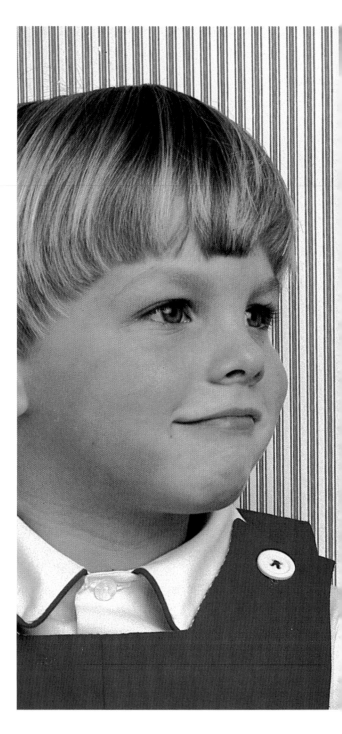

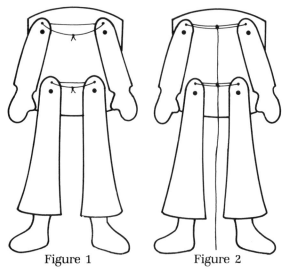

Figure 1   Figure 2

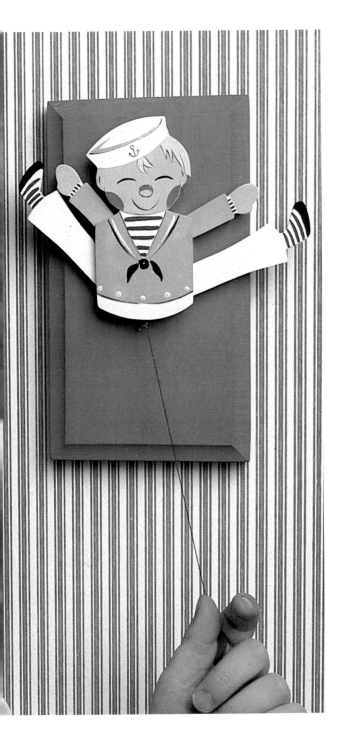

jumping jack on a plaque, drill a hole (with an ⅛″ drill bit) at "X" on pattern front.

Sand all the pieces until smooth. Paint the face and hat on front of body. (Do not paint the rest of body until sailor is assembled.) Paint arms and legs on both sides and on the edges. Paint the edges of the back and front. If you are going to mount the sailor, paint the plaque. If he will be an ornament, paint the back.

Cut four ½″-long pieces from the ⅛″-diameter dowels. Dip each end of each dowel in glue and insert in dowel holes on back; push dowel in as far as it will go. Place the arms on the dowels (thumbs in). Thread an 8″ length of heavy thread up from the back of the arms through the thread holes, and tie in center with a square knot. Cut off ends of thread. Do same for legs. (See Figure 1.) Using about 12″ of thread, tie first to arm threads, then to leg threads, and allow to hang down below feet. (Figure 2.) Put a dot of glue on each knot to prevent slippage.

Smear dowel ends with glue. Lining up dowels and holes, place front on dowels, and press downward until dowel ends are even with front. Be sure that there is enough room between front and back to allow free movement of arms and

legs. Sand dowel ends flush with the surface of the front and back. Finish painting the front section, painting over dowel ends. Attach small button or slice of dowel to end of thread. If you want to mount the jumping jack, glue the back to the plaque. If you prefer to let it hang as an ornament, make a loop and place a string through hole in the head.

A Little Lamb

This simple little lamb, with fleece of gathered eyelet, can be a tree ornament, a pet for a child's pocket, or an accent for a package.

MATERIALS:
   pattern on page 136
   ¼ yard white fabric
   scrap black fabric
   ½ yard narrow gathered eyelet
   polyester stuffing
   black and pink embroidery floss

Cut 2 bodies from white fabric. Cut 2 front and 2 back legs from black fabric. On both body pieces, satin stitch eyes and ears with black floss. On right side of one body, baste gathered eyelet around edges (except around nose and mouth), turning eyelet to inside. Machine stitch eyelet in place. On other piece, baste eyelet at tops of legs, and machine stitch. Place body pieces with right sides together and eyelet to inside. Baste, then stitch, leaving the bottom open. Turn and stuff. Place leg pieces right sides together and sew around edges except tops. Clip curves, turn, and stuff. Pin legs in place, turn seams inside, and whipstitch bottom of lamb. Use satin and straight stitches in pink floss for nose and mouth, working across seam. Loosely loop several strands of black floss to form the tail.

Sweet Baby, Sleep

As gentle as a lullaby, this painting in thread of Mary and her Baby was inspired by a favorite Christmas card. The simple design is skillfully suggested with only a minimum of stitches. Choose a good grade of felt, at least 50% wool, for the embroidery and its background; metallic gold sewing thread will add just the right accent for the design.

MATERIALS:
   pattern on page 141
   12″ square of white felt of good quality
   12″ × 16″ blue felt of good quality
   tissue paper
   crayons for coloring face: fluorescent
      pink and orange
   embroidery floss in brown, flesh, red,
      light blue, medium blue (the medium
      blue should match the blue felt
      background as closely as possible)
   metallic gold thread for hand sewing
   white sewing thread
   small amount of quilt batting or polyester
      stuffing
   frame, about 7″ × 9½″

Transfer the design to the white felt by tracing the design onto tissue paper, pinning the tissue to the felt, and basting along the lines of the design with basting stitches about ¼″ long. Gently tear away the tissue.

Color the faces and hands with crayons, coloring a little darker than you really want the flesh to appear because some of the color will be lost with the stitching.

As you stitch the design, remove basting stitches. Work all stitches with 1-ply floss unless otherwise directed.

Add facial features. Work eyelashes in straight stitches (brown), eyebrows in small fly stitches (brown), nose in a tiny straight stitch (brown), and mouth in a fly stitch (red). Outline face with tiny running stitches in flesh-colored floss.

Work the hair in outline stitch with 2-ply floss (brown), with rows placed closely together.

Work the child's body in satin stitch, using 2-ply floss (light blue). Make a tiny straight stitch for eye (brown), and outline face with tiny running stitches in flesh-colored floss.

Stitch halos with outlines of chain stitch, then with straight stitches (gold metallic thread).

Work inside of veil in satin stitch with 2-ply floss (medium blue). Chain stitch neckline (medium blue). Work shading under arm and under child's body with straight stitch (light blue). Make a few straight stitches (flesh) to suggest fingers.

For folds in dress and veil, make small running stitches with 1-ply floss (light blue).

When stitching is complete, cut out the design very carefully, allowing ⅛″ margin. Cut batting to shape but slightly smaller. Place the batting beneath the design, pin to blue background felt, and appliqué with tiny blind stitches in white sewing thread. Frame.

MATERIALS:

plastic foam cylinder (3″ diameter for large drums, 1½″ diameter for small drums)
emery board
velvet ribbon (1½″ wide for large drums, ⅞″ wide for small drums)
gold beads
gold cord
straight pins
white household glue
cotton swabs
black India ink, paint, or felt marker

Cut the cylinder into slices that are just a little wider than your ribbon (1″ for small drums, 1¾″ for large drums). Use an emery board to smooth the edges of the cylinder.

Cut a length of ribbon to go around the cylinder and overlap slightly. Place ribbon around cylinder, and push straight pins through ribbon into cylinder to hold in place.

Insert 3 straight pins through gold beads. Place these around one side of the ribbon, spacing the 3 equally around the cylinder. Insert 3 more straight pins through gold beads, and place them on the other side of the drum, also equally spaced, but with the pins halfway between the pins on the opposite side of the ribbon (see photograph).

Wrap cord around drum, going from the outside of a bead on one side to the outside of a bead on the other side, and continuing around the drum. When you again reach the starting point, hold the cord in place, remove the pin, and reinsert it through the cord to hold both ends of cord in place. Cut cord ends to 3″, and knot together to form a loop for hanging.

Color the cotton swabs with the India ink, paint, or marker. Allow to dry completely. Glue the swabs to drum, crossing them as shown in the photograph.

Rat-a-tat-tat

To keep your drummers drumming, provide them with these colorful drums that are simply constructed from plastic foam, ribbon, beads, and cord. The red, white, and gold colors are just right on a green tree, and the cotton-swab drumsticks add the finishing touch.

Children's Workshop
Twigs & Flowers

Twig baskets are shaped around juice cans to hold flowers that are made from the red shells of the pistachio nut. Little fingers can slip twigs around a juice can because rubber bands help to hold the twigs in place. A child may want to make just the basket and fill it with holly or flowers. A small bottle, such as a vitamin bottle, will slip into the basket so it can hold a bouquet of fresh flowers.

MATERIALS:
  For the basket:
  juice can
  brown paper
  2 rubber bands
  white household glue
  twigs
  honeysuckle vines
  For flowers:
  lightweight cardboard
  pipe cleaners or wires
  pistachio shells
  white household glue
  unpopped popcorn
  brown artist's acrylic or tempera paints
  (optional)

For the basket: Cut brown paper and wrap it around the outside of the can so the bright colors of the label will not show through. Glue in place. Slip 2 rubber bands around the can, one near the top and one near the bottom. To form a handle, cut 2 honeysuckle vines 20″ long. Wrap another long vine around and around the two vines. Slip the ends of the handles underneath the rubber bands. Glue the vines to the outside of the can.

Break twigs to the height of the can. Slip the twigs beneath the rubber bands until the can is covered all the way around. Leave the rubber bands in place. Wrap a long vine over the rubber bands. Tuck both ends of the vine beneath the wraps of vine.

For the flowers: Cut a circle of cardboard about the size of a quarter. Glue pistachio nut shells around the cardboard for petals. Glue the popcorn in the center. Stems from pipe cleaners can be made to look very much like twigs by dipping them into thinned brown artist's acrylic paint or tempera paints and allowing them to dry, or the pipe cleaners can be used plain. To attach the flowers to the pipe cleaner stems, simply curl one end of the pipe cleaner into a circle and glue circle to the back of a finished flower. Older children (old enough not to hurt themselves with wires) may prefer to use florist's wires to make less obtrusive stems for the flowers. If this is the case, the wire should be attached before the flower petals are glued on. Push about 2″ of a florist's wire to the top of the cardboard, form a "U," and push the wire back through a second hole. Twist the short end of the wire around the long wire. Then glue on the petals and popcorn.

Baskets for Your Tree

Simple folds in a triangle of wrapping paper will make these colorful baskets for the tree. Trims include self-stick, no-lick holiday stickers, bits of cord, and bright tissue paper.

MATERIALS:
  gift wrap in bright colors
  cord or ribbon for handle
  white household glue
  self-stick stickers
  tissue paper
  various fillers

Cut a 10″ square of the gift wrap; this will make two baskets. Cut the square into two equal triangles as shown in Figure 1. Fold one of the triangles as shown in the three steps of Figure 2. Cut across the folds as shown by the broken line across the folded paper in the last drawing.

Unfold the paper and shape into a four-sided basket. (Change directions on some of the folds to make all the creases work in the same direction.) You will see that there are two thicknesses of paper on each of the four sides. Glue the ends of an 8″ length of cord or ribbon between the layers on opposite sides of the basket. Glue the last outside panel into place. Allow the glue to dry thoroughly. Add tissue paper and fillers.

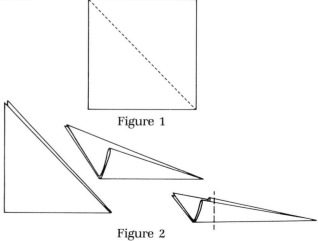

Figure 1

Figure 2

A Shining Star

Twinkle! Twinkle! Golden stars that glisten and shine. Children can make these star baskets for the tree, for gifts, or just for the fun of it!

MATERIALS:
   pattern on page 135
   gold wrapping paper
   typing paper
   white household glue

Use the small star on page 135 as a pattern. Trace the patterns for the star and handle onto typing paper. Cut out the typing paper patterns. Trace around the patterns on gold wrapping paper. For one star basket, cut 2 stars and one handle from the gold wrapping paper.

Place the stars with the back of the paper turned up. Glue the handle to both stars as shown in the diagram. Squeeze glue on one of the stars to make a line like the dotted line in the diagram. Fold the handle and place the two stars together, so they are glued around the bottom edges but will open at the top. After the glue is thoroughly dried, fill the baskets with flowers or candies.

Bulletin Boards to Give

On a rainy Saturday afternoon before Christmas, children will enjoy creating these bulletin boards as gifts for family and friends. Mother will need to help with cutting the plastic foam rectangles to size. Older children can then cut pieces from felt. Check packing materials in arriving packages to see if there are free rectangles of plastic foam to use as bases for the bulletin boards. Gather remnants and blocks of felt, scraps of lace, snips of rickrack, and bits of ribbon. Patterns are given for the designs shown here, but children are sure to add their own.

MATERIALS:
>   **patterns on pages 144-145**
>   **plastic foam rectangles (1″ thick) in**
>   **various sizes**
>   **fabric to cover the rectangles**
>   **white household glue**
>   **remnants of fabric, ribbon, lace, and**
>   **other trims**
>   **felt in various colors**

Place the plastic foam on a piece of fabric. Cut the fabric large enough to cover the front and sides and wrap around to the back of the block.

On the front of the plastic foam, run a line of glue around the edges. Place the fabric, right side up, on the rectangle and check to be sure stripes are straight and the fabric is placed just the way you want it. While the glue is still wet, the fabric can be shifted to straighten it. When the fabric on the front is correct, turn over the bulletin board. Run a line of glue around the sides of the bulletin board, and smooth the fabric toward the back. Now, run a line of glue on the back—around the edges—and pull the fabric onto the back and press with your hands until smooth. Allow the glue to dry.

When the glue is dry, turn the bulletin board right side up and glue on your decorations.

For the present: Wrap a ribbon across the top and to the back. Glue in place. Wrap another ribbon at the side to cross the first ribbon, and glue in place. Tie a pretty bow, and glue it where the ribbons cross.

For the sailboat: Trace the patterns and cut the pieces from felt. Make a line for the water with rickrack. Glue the boat just above the water. Glue on the sail and a mast of rickrack. Add a friend's name by spelling it in rickrack.

For the flower girl: Trace the patterns and cut pieces from felt. Glue the dress and face in place. Glue the hat so it overlaps onto the face, and add lace and rickrack for trims. Glue the apron in place. Add the arm. Glue lace around the skirt. Place flowers where you like. Cut letters from felt to write a name.

The patterns for the hammer and nail are also given. Cut them from felt, and add a name.

Place the 2 threads together and knot each end to hold them together. Wrap these threads around the middle of the shorter threads, and tie in a knot. (Figure 2.) Hold the long threads and pull the short threads down. Wrap another thread around the cluster and tie in a knot. (Figure 3.)

Spread glue lightly over the construction paper shape, and glue the painted gingerbread man on top, sandwiching the tassel cord between the two layers.

Figure 1

Figure 2

Figure 3

Mark Your Place

Felt-tip markers will help to turn the drawing of a gingerbread man into bookmarks for friends. Tie on a tassel made from many-colored threads.

MATERIALS:
typing paper
construction paper
felt-tip markers
embroidery floss
white household glue

Trace the gingerbread man onto the typing paper, and color him with the markers. Cut out the gingerbread man.

Trace just the outside lines of the gingerbread man onto typing paper. Cut out this tracing, and trace around it on the construction paper. Cut out the gingerbread man's shape.

To make the tassel, cut about 18 threads that are 6″ long. Place all the threads together with the ends even. (Figure 1.) Cut 2 threads 10″ long.

A Christmas Twirler

Twirl this toy and watch Santa hop into his sleigh and the reindeer gallop through the air. When the twirler spins fast enough, the two images of Santa and his sleigh blend together to put Santa inside the sleigh. The legs of the reindeer—in first one position, then another, and back again—seem to move, and he runs faster and faster as the twirler goes around.

MATERIALS:
> **typing paper**
> **black pen**
> **small piece of cardboard**
> **white household glue**
> **2 (12″-long) strings**

Trace the two sides of the twirler shown at right (including the lines around the outside). With the pen, darken in all the areas that are dark on the drawings.

Cut one piece of cardboard exactly the same size as the block made by the outside lines of the twirler. Cut out the sides of the twirler that you have drawn on the typing paper, cutting just outside the black lines.

Glue the two pictures you have drawn on the sides of the cardboard, with the reindeer *upside down* on one side and *right side up* on the other.

Attach the strings at the sides, and twirl strings between your fingers as shown in the drawing below.

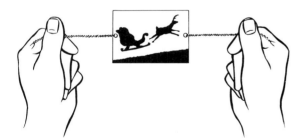

78

Wraps

Baskets for the Bath

Pretty baskets for pretty presents. These easy-to-make baskets will hold soaps and colognes, bath oils, sponges, and other gifts for a lady's dressing room and bath. Select the fragrances and colors you know she will like, and make a special basket in her favorite colors.

MATERIALS:
  baskets in assorted sizes and types
  gathered lace, about 2″ wide and long
    enough to go around basket
  white household glue
  metallic enamel spray paint
  ribbon (optional)

Mix a small amount of glue with an equal amount of water. Cut lace to a length that will go around the top of the basket.

Saturate the lace with the glue mixture. Press the lace between your fingers to remove excessive glue that would drip, but do not squeeze or crumple the lace more than necessary.

Run a thin line of undiluted glue around the edge of the basket. Wrap the saturated lace around the basket, and place three or four clothespins around the basket to hold the top of the lace in place. Allow to dry overnight or until lace is dry and stiff.

Spray paint the basket and lace. Apply two or more light coats rather than one heavy coat that would drip and run along the edges of the lace. Add ribbon if you like, and fill with gift items.

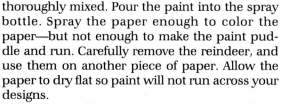

Reindeer Parcels

Reindeer bound through wintry night skies to transform your Christmas wraps from brown paper and unbleached muslin to handmade papers and bags. The technique is so easy that you will wonder why you never did it before. Save brown sacks, not quite as heavy as grocery bags, to make these gift papers that proudly announce that you made it yourself. Sew a reindeer bag to hold those strangely shaped gifts that will never fit into a box. Fill a bag with kindling for fire-loving friends, or pack a coloring book and crayons into a "going-away" bag for your favorite small holiday visitor.

MATERIALS:
> **pattern on page 145**
> **lightweight cardboard (such as a manila folder)**
> **brown paper**
> **unbleached muslin**
> **artist's acrylic tube paints**
> **small spray bottle**
> **white sewing thread**
> **jute or similar cord for drawstrings and ties**
> **small weights (such as nuts and bolts)**

Place old newspaper on the floor to make the cleanup easy.

For the paper: Trace reindeer pattern and cut several reindeer from lightweight cardboard. Place brown paper on the newspaper. Arrange the reindeer on the brown paper, and place the small weights in the center of the reindeer. The weights are necessary because the cardboard will curl as it becomes wet, and you will lose the sharp lines of the design unless you weight the reindeer each time they are used.

Mix 3 tablespoons of artist's acrylics with 3 tablespoons of water in a small dish. Stir until thoroughly mixed. Pour the paint into the spray bottle. Spray the paper enough to color the paper—but not enough to make the paint puddle and run. Carefully remove the reindeer, and use them on another piece of paper. Allow the paper to dry flat so paint will not run across your designs.

For the muslin bags: Cut 2 pieces of muslin (a front and a back) the size you want your bag to be, allowing for a seam on all sides. (The bags shown here measure about 10″ × 12″ and 7″ × 11″.) Put aside the back of the bag; it remains unpainted.

Paint the fronts of the bags, using the same method as given for the paper.

After the bag is thoroughly dry, place front and back of bag with right sides together. Sew sides and bottom of bag. Make a casing at the top. Turn bag right side out, and insert drawstring.

Clearly a Present

Wraps should not always conceal the present. Let your prettiest gifts show in these Plexiglas® boxes. Here, Christmas treats are shown to their best advantage. Imagine, too, the boxes filled with hair ribbons or toy soldiers or a special present, perhaps jewelry, hidden in a beautiful scarf. These inexpensive and easy-to-find boxes become a part of the gift!

Celebrations from the Kitchen

Every Christmas, it seems, is a little like all the other Christmases we have known. Our favorite cake smells wonderfully spicy and buttery—just as it has smelled for all our other Christmases. Christmas foods, like many other Christmas customs, combine our very latest and best approaches to our oldest and most treasured traditions. This year, for example, try Baked Alaska Mincemeat Pie, which combines packaged mincemeat with ice cream beneath a just-baked meringue in an impressive but easy-to-make dessert. On Christmas Eve of 1666, though, the wife of diarist Samuel Pepys was up until four in the morning to supervise her maids as they made mince pies. Many legends surround this traditional dessert that is known as Christmas Pie. (Remember Jack Horner?) The Puritans banned mince pies along with other "sinful" Christmas merrymaking. On the other hand, it was long a tradition to eat mince pie on each of the twelve days of Christmas to assure good fortune throughout the coming year.

In this chapter, you will find many other new recipes to add to your traditional favorites. Fruity breads, hard candies, and spicy, hot beverages. Cheesecake and fruitcake and coconut cake. Foods to serve at parties and food to give as gifts. And the cookies on the cover? The recipes are here.

Merry Christmas cooking. Happy memory making. And may you enjoy your Christmas Pie.

Cookies

As Christmas as cookies! So much a part of the Christmas tradition, cookies have long been used as both decoration and food for the holiday season. You will find cookies throughout *Christmas with Southern Living 1983.*

A cookie, carefully decorated, becomes the perfect napkin accent for a Christmas table. Introduce the holiday meal with the wreath shown at right. Cookies become candleholders (page 52) as stars are cut from purchased dough and stacked three deep to surround a candle. (Our instructions include the easy way to cut the center hole for the candle.)

Cookies are used on a Christmas tree—and some more permanent "cookies" are shaped from felt to last from year to year. Icing, candies, and sprinkles on real cookies are translated into rickrack, beads, and buttons on felt sugarplums. Mix real cookies and felt versions on a Cookie Tree (page 27), or make felt cookies for the tree and prepare real cookies (using the same cookie cutters) in clear wrap to present as favors to admirers of the tree. And be sure to bedeck the tree skirt with more cookie shapes.

Of course, the very best thing to do with a cookie is to eat it. The cookies that decorate our cover and the introductions to the chapters of the book are all made from recipes given in this chapter. For the decorated cookies, we used cutters that are readily available, but these should be only a beginning for your own designs. Bring out your own cookie cutters and add more designs to the collection. The "packages" on the cover, for example, need no cutter; they are simply rectangles with ribbons of icing.

Introduce a Christmas meal with a napkin holder that is a cookie wreath with leaves, berries, and ribbon of piped icing.

All the decorated cookies are made from four recipes. Cut gingerbread men or reindeer from Gingerbread Cookies, Sour Cream Cookies, or Butter Pecan Shortbread Cookies. Use a single recipe for all the cookie shapes, or try all the recipes. Press wreaths and trees from Cream Cheese Spritz. Two icing recipes are given. Royal Icing is a harder, more lasting icing that is especially good for cookies that you want to use as

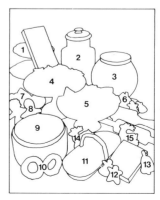

Treat your family to the season's most spectacular cookies: 1, 9, 10 Cream Cheese Spritz; 2 Double Treat Cookies; 3 Christmas Crunchies; 4 Butter Pecan Shortbread; 5, 7, 11, 13, 14, 15 Sour Cream Cookies; 6, 8, 12 Gingerbread Cookies

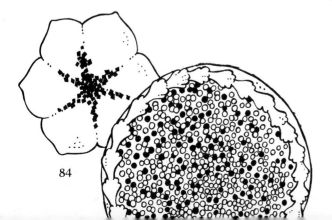

84

decorations or to display in any way. Decorator Icing is softer, good for cookies that you won't need to stack or to keep for a long time. Besides the decorated cookies, there are others just as good. Try pretty Jam Kolaches; Double Chocolate Bars; Christmas Crunchies made with coconut, pecans, and oats; Double Treat Cookies, drop cookies with chocolate morsels; and those all-time favorites, Christmas Fruitcake Cookies.

Solve problems from your gift list with cookies. As favors for a children's party, package cookies in clear wrap and add a perky bow or party-favor streamers. And lucky is the person who is presented with a sampling of several types of cookies. Cookies will please sophisticated friends and bouncing four-year-olds alike.

Bring out the rolling pin and cookie cutters, assemble the ingredients, perhaps add a friend to share the baking, and have fun!

Decorating tip—A drop of light corn syrup will hold decorator candies in place on the cookies.

DECORATOR ICING

- ¼ cup butter, softened
- 2 cups powdered sugar, sifted
- 2 tablespoons milk
- ½ teaspoon vanilla extract
  Red or green paste food coloring (optional)

Cream butter; gradually add sugar, beating well. Add milk and vanilla, mixing until smooth. Color portions of icing with paste food coloring, if desired. Prepare decorating bags, and decorate as desired. (This icing stays soft and moist; do not stack cookies.) Yield: about 1 cup.

86

ROYAL ICING

- 3 large egg whites
- ½ teaspoon cream of tartar
- 1 (16-ounce) package powdered sugar, sifted
  Red and green paste food coloring (optional)

Combine egg whites (at room temperature) and cream of tartar in a large mixing bowl. Beat at medium speed with an electric mixer until frothy. Gradually add powdered sugar, mixing well. Beat 5 to 7 minutes. Color portions of icing with paste food coloring, if desired. Prepare decorating bags, and decorate as desired. (Icing dries very quickly; keep covered at all times with plastic wrap.) Yield: about 2 cups.

Note: Royal Icing dries very hard and is used for making decorations to last indefinitely. It is edible, but crunchy. Most cookies are decorated with Royal Icing.

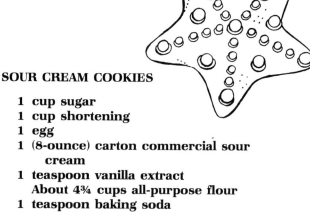

SOUR CREAM COOKIES

- 1 cup sugar
- 1 cup shortening
- 1 egg
- 1 (8-ounce) carton commercial sour cream
- 1 teaspoon vanilla extract
  About 4¾ cups all-purpose flour
- 1 teaspoon baking soda
- 1 teaspoon baking powder
- ¼ teaspoon salt
  Red and green decorator sugar crystals (optional)
  Decorator Icing or Royal Icing (optional)
  Assorted candies and sprinkles (optional)

Combine first 3 ingredients; beat until light and fluffy. Stir in sour cream and vanilla, mixing well. Combine flour, baking soda, baking powder, and salt; add to creamed mixture, beating well. Chill dough at least 1 hour.

Divide dough into thirds; work with one-third of dough at a time, keeping remaining dough refrigerated. Roll out dough onto a lightly floured surface to ⅛-inch thickness; cut into desired shapes. Place cookies on ungreased cookie sheets; sprinkle with sugar crystals, if desired. Bake at 350° for 10 to 12 minutes or until lightly browned. Remove from pan and cool on wire racks. Decorate as desired with icing (page 86) and assorted candies and sprinkles. Yield: about 8 dozen (3-inch) cookies.

BUTTER PECAN SHORTBREAD COOKIES

  1 **cup butter, softened**
  ½ **cup firmly packed brown sugar**
2¼ **cups all-purpose flour**
  ½ **cup finely chopped pecans**
    Decorator Icing or Royal Icing
    (optional)
    Assorted candies and sprinkles
    (optional)

Cream butter; gradually add sugar, beating until light and fluffy. Gradually add flour, mixing well. Stir in pecans. Divide dough in half, and chill at least 1 hour.

Roll 1 portion of dough to ¼-inch thickness between sheets of waxed paper; keep remaining dough chilled until ready to use. Remove top sheet of waxed paper. Cut dough into desired shapes; remove excess dough. Place greased cookie sheet on top of cookies; invert and remove waxed paper.

Bake at 300° for 18 to 20 minutes or until lightly browned. Remove immediately to wire racks to cool. Repeat with remaining dough. Decorate as desired with icing (page 86) and assorted candies and sprinkles. Yield: about 3 dozen (3-inch) cookies.

GINGERBREAD COOKIES

  ½ **cup butter or margarine, softened**
  ½ **cup firmly packed brown sugar**
  ½ **cup molasses**
  1 **egg**
3½ **cups all-purpose flour**
  1 **teaspoon baking powder**
  ½ **teaspoon baking soda**
  ½ **teaspoon salt**
  1 **teaspoon ground cinnamon**
  ½ **teaspoon ground ginger**
  ¼ **teaspoon ground nutmeg**
  ¼ **teaspoon ground cloves**
  ½ **cup buttermilk**
    Raisins (optional)
    Decorator Icing or Royal Icing
    (optional)
    Assorted candies and sprinkles
    (optional)

Cream butter; add sugar and beat until light and fluffy. Add molasses and egg; mix well. Combine dry ingredients; add to creamed mixture alternately with buttermilk, beginning and ending with dry ingredients. Shape dough into a ball; cover and chill at least 2 hours.

Roll out dough onto a lightly floured surface to ¼-inch thickness; cut into desired shapes. Place on lightly greased cookie sheets; decorate with raisins, if desired. Bake at 375° for 10 minutes. Remove from pan and cool on wire racks. Decorate as desired with icing (page 86) and assorted candies and sprinkles. Yield: about 3 dozen (3-inch) cookies.

JAM KOLACHES

½ cup butter or margarine, softened
1 (3-ounce) package cream cheese, softened
1¼ cups all-purpose flour
About ¼ cup strawberry jam
¼ cup sifted powdered sugar

Cream butter and cream cheese; beat until light and fluffy. Add flour, mixing well.

Roll out dough onto a lightly floured surface to ⅛-inch thickness; cut into rounds with a 2-inch cookie cutter. Place on lightly greased cookie sheets. Spoon ¼ teaspoon jam on each cookie; fold in opposite sides, slightly overlapping edges. Bake at 375° for 15 minutes. Remove from cookie sheets, and sprinkle with powdered sugar. Yield: about 2 dozen.

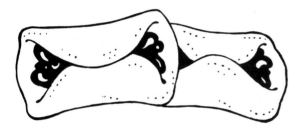

CHRISTMAS FRUITCAKE COOKIES

1 cup butter, softened
1½ cups sugar
2 eggs
2½ cups all-purpose flour
½ teaspoon salt
1 teaspoon baking soda
1 teaspoon ground cinnamon
2 (8-ounce) packages chopped pitted dates
3 cups chopped pecans
1 (8-ounce) package candied yellow pineapple, chopped
1 (8-ounce) package candied red cherries, cut into quarters

Cream butter; gradually add sugar, beating until light and fluffy. Add eggs, and beat well. Combine flour, salt, baking soda, and cinnamon; gradually add to creamed mixture, beating well after each addition. Stir in the remaining ingredients.

Drop dough by heaping teaspoonfuls onto lightly greased cookie sheets. Bake at 375° for 13 minutes or until lightly browned. Cool on cookie sheets about 1 minute; remove cookies to wire racks, and cool completely. Yield: about 7 dozen.

CREAM CHEESE SPRITZ

1 cup butter or margarine, softened
1 (8-ounce) package cream cheese, softened
⅔ cup sugar
1 teaspoon vanilla extract
2 cups all-purpose flour
Dash of salt
Red and green decorator sugar crystals (optional)
Decorator Icing or Royal Icing (optional)
Assorted candies and sprinkles (optional)

Cream butter and cream cheese; add sugar and beat until light and fluffy. Add vanilla and mix well. Combine flour and salt; gradually add to creamed mixture, beating well after each addition. Shape dough into a ball and chill thoroughly.

Place dough into a cookie press with desired disc; press cookies onto ungreased cookie sheets. Sprinkle with sugar crystals, if desired. Bake at 400° for 8 to 10 minutes or until very lightly browned. Remove from pan and cool on wire racks. Decorate as desired with icing (page 86) and assorted candies and sprinkles. Yield: about 4 dozen (2-inch) cookies.

Christmas Fruitcake Cookies (left) and Jam Kolaches are easy to make, yet taste good.

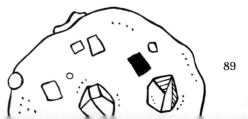

CHRISTMAS CRUNCHIES

½ cup butter or margarine, softened
½ cup sugar
½ cup firmly packed brown sugar
1 egg
½ teaspoon vanilla extract
1 cup all-purpose flour
½ teaspoon baking soda
¼ teaspoon baking powder
¼ teaspoon salt
1 cup regular oats, uncooked
1 cup corn flakes
½ cup shredded coconut
½ cup coarsely chopped pecans

Cream butter; add sugar, and beat until light and fluffy. Add egg and vanilla, mixing well. Combine flour, baking soda, baking powder, and salt; gradually add to creamed mixture, beating well after each addition. Stir in oats, corn flakes, coconut, and pecans.

Shape dough into 1-inch balls and place 2-inches apart on lightly greased cookie sheets. Bake at 350° for 10 to 12 minutes. Cool on wire racks. Yield: about 3½ dozen.

DOUBLE CHOCOLATE BARS

1 (18.5-ounce) package devil's food cake mix without pudding
½ cup butter or margarine, melted
2 eggs
1 (8-ounce) package cream cheese, softened
¼ cup sugar
1 teaspoon vanilla extract
1 cup flaked coconut
1 (6-ounce) package semisweet chocolate morsels
½ cup finely chopped pecans

Combine cake mix, butter, and 1 egg; beat at low speed with an electric mixer until smooth. Reserve ⅔ cup mixture; set aside. Press remaining cake mixture into a greased 13- x 9- x 2-inch baking pan. Bake at 350° for 15 minutes.

Combine cream cheese, sugar, vanilla, and 1 egg; beat at low speed with an electric mixer until smooth. Stir in coconut and chocolate morsels. Spread coconut mixture evenly over crust. Add pecans to reserved cake mixture; sprinkle over filling. Bake at 350° for 20 to 25 minutes. Cool in pan and cut into bars. Yield: 4½ dozen.

DOUBLE TREAT COOKIES

½ cup softened margarine or shortening
½ cup crunchy peanut butter
½ cup firmly packed brown sugar
½ cup sugar
1 egg
½ teaspoon vanilla extract
1¼ cups all-purpose flour
1 teaspoon baking soda
¼ teaspoon salt
1 (6-ounce) package semisweet chocolate morsels

Cream margarine and peanut butter; gradually add sugar, beating until light and fluffy. Add the egg and vanilla; beat well. Combine dry ingredients; add to creamed mixture, mixing well. Stir in chocolate morsels.

Drop dough by rounded teaspoonfuls onto ungreased cookie sheets. Bake at 350° for 8 to 10 minutes. Remove to wire racks to cool. Yield: about 4½ dozen.

PEANUT BUTTER FINGERS

1 cup all-purpose flour
½ cup sugar
½ cup firmly packed brown sugar
½ teaspoon baking soda
¼ teaspoon salt
½ cup butter or margarine, softened
⅓ cup crunchy peanut butter
1 egg
1 cup regular oats, uncooked
1 (12-ounce) package semisweet
    chocolate morsels
½ cup sifted powdered sugar
¼ cup crunchy peanut butter
2 to 4 tablespoons milk

Combine first 9 ingredients in a large mixing bowl; mix well.

Press dough into a greased 13- × 9- × 2-inch pan. Bake at 350° for 20 minutes. Remove from oven, and sprinkle with chocolate morsels. Let stand 5 minutes or until melted; spread evenly. Combine powdered sugar, ¼ cup peanut butter, and milk; beat well. Drizzle over cookies. Cut into bars. Yield: 2½ dozen.

HONEY-OATMEAL COOKIES

1 cup butter or margarine, softened
1 cup sugar
¼ cup honey
2 eggs
½ cup commercial sour cream
2 cups all-purpose flour
1 teaspoon salt
1 teaspoon baking soda
1 teaspoon ground cinnamon
1 teaspoon ground ginger
3 cups quick-cooking oats, uncooked
1 cup chopped dates

Cream butter; gradually add sugar and honey, beating until light and fluffy. Add eggs, one at a time, beating well after each addition. Add sour cream, and mix well.

Combine flour, salt, soda, cinnamon, and ginger; add to creamed mixture. Stir in oats and dates, mixing well.

Drop dough by teaspoonfuls onto greased cookie sheets; bake at 375° for 10 to 12 minutes. Cool 5 minutes before removing from cookie sheets. Yield: about 8 dozen.

WHOLE WHEAT-WALNUT COOKIES

½ cup shortening
1 cup sugar
2 eggs, well beaten
1 teaspoon vanilla extract
1¾ cups whole wheat flour
¼ teaspoon baking soda
¼ teaspoon salt
½ cup finely chopped black walnuts

Cream shortening; gradually add sugar, beating until light and fluffy. Beat in eggs and vanilla. Combine remaining ingredients, and stir into creamed mixture. Chill dough 2 hours or until dough is stiff.

Shape dough into a long roll 2½ inches in diameter; wrap in waxed paper, and chill 3 to 4 hours. Cut into ¼-inch slices; place on ungreased cookie sheets. Bake at 400° for 6 to 8 minutes. Yield: about 5 dozen.

Beverages

CHRISTMAS BUTTERED BRANDY

- 1 cup butter, softened
- ½ cup firmly packed brown sugar
- ½ cup sifted powdered sugar
- 1 teaspoon ground nutmeg
- 1 teaspoon ground cinnamon
- 1 pint vanilla ice cream, softened
  Brandy
  Whipped cream (optional)
  Cinnamon sticks (optional)

Combine butter, sugar, and spices; beat until light and fluffy. Add ice cream, and stir until well blended. Spoon mixture into a 2-quart freezer-proof container; freeze.

Thaw slightly to serve. Place 3 tablespoons butter mixture and 1 ounce of brandy in a large mug; fill with boiling water, stirring well. (Any unused butter mixture can be refrozen.) Top with whipped cream, and serve with cinnamon stick, if desired. Yield: about 12 cups.

MILK PUNCH

- 1 (4/5-quart) bottle bourbon
- 3 quarts half-and-half
- ¼ cup vanilla extract
  Simple syrup (recipe follows)
  Ground nutmeg

Combine bourbon, half-and-half, and vanilla in a 1-gallon container; add simple syrup to desired sweetness. Chill thoroughly. Sprinkle with nutmeg before serving. Yield: 1 gallon.

Simple Syrup:

- 1 cup sugar
- 1 cup water

Combine sugar and water in a small saucepan; boil 5 minutes. Cool completely before using. Yield: 1¼ cups.

HOSPITALITY PUNCH

- ¾ cup lemon juice
- ½ cup plus 2 tablespoons brandy
- ⅓ cup maraschino cherry juice
- ¼ cup plus 2 tablespoons curaçao
- ¼ cup sugar
- 4 (25.4-ounce) bottles champagne, chilled
- 2 (32-ounce) bottles tonic water, chilled

Combine first 5 ingredients, stirring until sugar dissolves. Pour over ice in punch bowl; add champagne and tonic water just before serving. Yield: 5 quarts.

HOLIDAY CHEER

- 2 (25.4-ounce) bottles rosé, chilled
- 1 pint port
- 1 cup cherry brandy
- ½ cup superfine sugar
  Juice of 2 lemons
  Juice of 2 oranges
- 1 (32-ounce) bottle club soda, chilled

Combine all ingredients except club soda; mix well until sugar dissolves. Add club soda just before serving. Serve beverage over crushed ice. Yield: 3 quarts.

Greet your guests with a pitcher of refreshing Holiday Cheer.

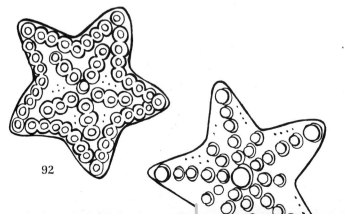

ORANGE WASSAIL

1 cup sugar
1 cup water
1 dozen whole cloves
2 (2-inch) sticks cinnamon
3 quarts orange juice
1 (32-ounce) bottle cranberry juice
    cocktail

Combine sugar, water, and spices in a large Dutch oven; simmer over low heat 10 minutes. Discard spices. Add juices to syrup; heat well. Yield: 4 quarts.

PERKY CRANBERRY PUNCH

2 (32-ounce) bottles cranberry juice
    cocktail
1 (46-ounce) can unsweetened pineapple
    juice
2 cups water
1⅓ cups firmly packed brown sugar
2 tablespoons whole allspice
1 to 2 tablespoons whole cloves
12 (2-inch) sticks cinnamon

Pour cranberry juice, pineapple juice, water, and brown sugar into a 20-cup percolator; stir until sugar is dissolved. Place remaining ingredients in perculator basket. Perk through complete cycle of perculator. Serve hot. Yield: 16 cups.

HOLIDAY NOG

6 eggs, separated
¾ cup sugar, divided
⅛ teaspoon salt
2 cups whipping cream, whipped
2 cups milk
1 teaspoon vanilla extract
    Ground nutmeg

Combine egg yolks, ½ cup sugar, and salt in a large mixing bowl; beat at high speed with an electric mixer until thick and lemon colored.

Beat the egg whites (at room temperature) until foamy; gradually add the remaining ¼ cup sugar, 1 tablespoon at a time, beating until stiff peaks form.

Gently fold egg whites and next 3 ingredients into egg yolk mixture. Pour into a half-gallon container; store in refrigerator. Shake before serving, and sprinkle with nutmeg. Yield: about 1½ quarts.

Note: Scoops of vanilla ice cream may be floated on top.

SPICED MOCHA

½ cup whipping cream
1 tablespoon instant coffee granules
3 tablespoons sugar
½ teaspoon ground cinnamon
¼ teaspoon ground nutmeg
    Dash of ground cloves
¼ cup plus 2 tablespoons chocolate
    syrup, divided
    Hot coffee
6 cinnamon sticks (optional)

Combine first 6 ingredients; chill several hours. Beat at high speed with an electric mixer until soft peaks form.

Spoon 1 tablespoon chocolate syrup into each of 6 coffee mugs. Fill with hot coffee, stirring well. Top each with a generous spoonful of spiced whipped cream. Serve with cinnamon sticks, if desired. Yield: 6 servings.

Breads

CRANBERRY CRISSCROSS

- ½ cup boiling water
- 2 tablespoons butter or margarine
- 3 tablespoons sugar
- 1 package dry yeast
- 2 tablespoons warm water (105° to 115°)
- ½ teaspoon salt
- 1 egg
  About 2 cups all-purpose flour
  Cranberry Filling
  Glaze (recipe follows)

Combine boiling water, butter, and sugar in a small mixing bowl, stirring until sugar dissolves; set aside to cool.

Dissolve yeast in warm water in a large bowl. Add sugar mixture, salt, egg, and 1 cup flour; beat at low speed with an electric mixer until smooth. Stir in enough remaining flour to make a soft dough.

Place dough in a greased bowl, turning to grease top. Cover and refrigerate overnight or at least 12 hours.

Roll dough into a 15- x 8-inch rectangle on a lightly floured surface. Place rectangle on greased cookie sheet. Spoon Cranberry Filling down center of dough. Make 3-inch cuts at 1-inch intervals on each side. Crisscross strips from each side over filling, tucking in end of last one. Cover and let rise in a warm place (85°), free from drafts, 1 hour or until doubled in bulk. Bake at 375° for 20 minutes or until golden brown. Spread top with glaze while warm. Yield: 8 to 10 servings.

Cranberry Filling:

- 1 cup fresh cranberries
- ¼ cup water
- ½ cup sugar
- 1 tablespoon all-purpose flour
- 1 teaspoon grated orange rind

Combine cranberries and water in a saucepan; bring to a boil. Reduce heat; cover and cook 3 minutes over medium heat.

Combine sugar and flour; add to cranberries, stirring constantly. Cook over low heat until filling is thickened. Stir in orange rind. Cool. Yield: about ¾ cup.

Glaze:

- 1 cup sifted powdered sugar
- ½ teaspoon vanilla extract
- 2 tablespoons milk
  Dash of salt

Combine all ingredients in a small bowl; mix well. Yield: about ⅓ cup.

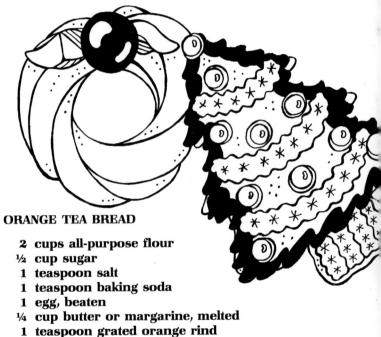

ORANGE TEA BREAD

- 2 cups all-purpose flour
- ½ cup sugar
- 1 teaspoon salt
- 1 teaspoon baking soda
- 1 egg, beaten
- ¼ cup butter or margarine, melted
- 1 teaspoon grated orange rind
- 1 teaspoon grated lemon rind
- 1 cup orange juice
- 1 cup chopped pecans

Combine flour, sugar, salt, and soda; add remaining ingredients, mixing well. Pour into a greased 9- × 5- × 3-inch loafpan. Bake at 350° for 50 minutes. Yield: 1 loaf.

LEMON BLOSSOM TWISTS

- 1 package dry yeast
- 3 tablespoons sugar
- ¼ cup warm water (105° to 115°)
- 1 egg
- ¾ cup commercial sour cream (at room temperature)
- About 2¾ cups all-purpose flour
- 1 teaspoon salt
- ⅛ teaspoon baking soda
- Lemon Blossom Filling
- Lemon Blossom Frosting

Dissolve yeast and sugar in warm water in a large bowl; add egg and sour cream, mixing well. Combine flour, salt, and baking soda; add to yeast mixture, mixing well.

Turn out dough onto a floured surface; roll to a 20- x 8-inch rectangle. Spread Lemon Blossom Filling lengthwise down center of rectangle. Fold long sides to center, slightly overlapping edges; cut into 4- x 1-inch strips. Twist each strip once, and place on greased baking sheets. Bake at 375° for 12 to 15 minutes. Frost with Lemon Blossom Frosting while warm. Yield: 20 rolls.

Lemon Blossom Filling:

- 1 (8-ounce) package cream cheese, softened
- 1 (3¾-ounce) package lemon instant pudding mix
- 2 tablespoons water
- 2 teaspoons lemon juice
- 1 egg

Combine all ingredients; stir until smooth. Yield: ⅔ cup.

Lemon Blossom Frosting:

- 1½ cups sifted powdered sugar
- 2 tablespoons lemon juice
- 1 tablespoon butter, softened

Combine all ingredients; stir until smooth. Yield: about ½ cup.

Welcome the season with the aroma and goodness of these home-baked breads. Top to bottom: Christmas Tea Ring, Brown Sugar Cinnamon Rolls, and Lemon Blossom Twists.

BROWN SUGAR CINNAMON ROLLS

- 2 packages dry yeast
- 1 cup warm water (105° to 115°)
- ½ cup shortening
- ½ cup butter or margarine, softened
- ¾ cup sugar
- 1 cup boiling water
- 2 eggs, well beaten
- 2 teaspoons salt
- About 6 cups all-purpose flour
- ¼ cup butter or margarine, softened
- ½ cup firmly packed brown sugar
- ½ cup chopped walnuts
- 1 teaspoon ground cinnamon

Dissolve yeast in 1 cup warm water, and set mixture aside.

Cream shortening and ½ cup butter; gradually add sugar and boiling water, beating well. Cool mixture to lukewarm (105° to 115°). Add the yeast mixture, eggs, salt, and 2 cups flour; beat at low speed with an electric mixer until smooth. Stir in enough of the remaining flour to make a soft dough. Place the dough in a greased bowl, turning to grease top. Cover and refrigerate dough overnight.

Roll dough to a 24- x 18-inch rectangle on a lightly floured surface; spread ¼ cup butter evenly over dough. Combine brown sugar, walnuts, and cinnamon; sprinkle over dough. Roll up dough, jellyroll fashion, beginning at long side; pinch edges to seal. Cut roll into 1-inch slices; place slices, cut side down, in greased muffin pans.

Cover and let rise in warm place (85°), free from drafts, about 1 hour or until doubled in bulk. Bake rolls at 375° for 20 to 25 minutes. Yield: 2 dozen.

CHRISTMAS TEA RING

>   2 packages dry yeast
> ½ cup warm water (105° to 115°)
> 1½ cups warm milk (105° to 115°)
> ½ cup sugar
>   2 teaspoons salt
>   2 eggs, beaten
> ½ cup vegetable oil
> 6½ to 7½ cups all-purpose flour
> ¼ cup butter or margarine, melted
> ½ cup sugar
>   1 tablespoon ground cinnamon
>   3 tablespoons raisins
>   3 tablespoons chopped candied cherries
>   3 tablespoons chopped pecans
>   1 cup sifted powdered sugar
>   2 tablespoons milk
>   Candied red cherries (optional)

Dissolve yeast in warm water in a large bowl; set aside 5 minutes. Add milk, ½ cup sugar, salt, eggs, oil, and half the flour; beat at low speed with an electric mixer until smooth. Stir in enough remaining flour to make a soft but slightly sticky dough.

Place dough in a greased bowl, turning to grease top. Cover and let rise in a warm place (85°), free from drafts, 1 hour or until dough is doubled in bulk.

Turn out dough onto a floured surface, and knead about 5 minutes until smooth and elastic. Return dough to bowl; cover and let rise in a warm place (85°), free from drafts, about 40 minutes or until doubled in bulk.

Divide dough in half. Roll each half of dough into a 21- x 7-inch rectangle on a lightly floured surface. Brush half of butter evenly over dough, leaving a 1-inch margin. Combine ½ cup sugar, cinnamon, raisins, cherries, and pecans; sprinkle half of mixture evenly over each rectangle, leaving a 1-inch margin. Roll up dough, jellyroll fashion, beginning at long side. Pinch edges to seal. Repeat procedure with remaining dough.

Place each roll on a large, greased baking sheet, seam side down; shape each into a ring, and pinch ends together to seal.

Using kitchen shears or a sharp knife, make cuts in dough every inch around rings, cutting two-thirds of the way through roll at each cut. Gently turn each piece of dough on its side, slightly overlapping slices. Cover and let rise in a warm place (85°), free from drafts, for 30 minutes or until doubled in bulk.

Bake at 350° for 25 to 30 minutes or until golden brown. Transfer to a wire rack. Cool. Combine powdered sugar and milk; drizzle glaze over ring. Garnish with candied cherries, if desired. Yield: 2 coffee cakes.

RAISIN CINNAMON ROLLS

>   About 3½ cups all-purpose flour,
>   divided
>   1 package dry yeast
> 1¼ cups milk
> ¼ cup sugar
> ¼ cup shortening
>   1 teaspoon salt
>   1 egg
> ½ cup sugar
> ¼ cup butter or margarine, melted
>   2 teaspoons ground cinnamon
> ½ cup raisins, divided
>   Glaze (recipe follows)

Combine 2 cups flour and yeast in a large bowl; stir well and set aside. Combine milk, ¼ cup sugar, shortening, and salt in a saucepan. Cook over medium heat until mixture reaches 120° to 130°. Pour into yeast mixture, mixing well. Add egg and mix at low speed with an electric mixer for 30 seconds; beat at high speed for 3 minutes, scraping sides of bowl.

Stir in remaining 1½ cups flour. Place dough in a greased bowl, turning to grease top. Cover and let rise in a warm place (85°), free from drafts, 1½ to 2 hours or until doubled in bulk.

Divide dough in half. Roll each half into a 16- x 8-inch rectangle on a lightly floured surface.

Combine ½ cup sugar, butter, and cinnamon; spread half of mixture over each rectangle and top each rectangle with ¼ cup of raisins. Roll up, jellyroll fashion, beginning with long side; pinch long edge (do not seal ends). Cut roll into 1-inch slices; place slices, cut side down, in 2 greased 9-inch square baking pans.

Cover and let rise in a warm place (85°), free from drafts, 1 hour or until doubled in bulk. Bake at 375° for 20 to 25 minutes. Drizzle with glaze while warm. Yield: 3 dozen.

Glaze:

- 1 cup sifted powdered sugar
- 1 to 2 tablespoons milk
- ½ teaspoon vanilla extract

Combine all ingredients; stir until smooth. Yield: about ⅓ cup.

BUTTER-RICH CRESCENT ROLLS

- 1 package dry yeast
- ¼ cup warm water (105° to 115°)
- ¼ cup sugar
- 1 teaspoon salt
- ¼ cup butter or margarine, softened
- 1 egg, beaten
- ¾ cup milk, scalded
  About 3 cups all-purpose flour
  Melted butter or margarine

Dissolve yeast in warm water in a large bowl. Add sugar, salt, butter, egg, milk, and 1½ cups flour; beat at low speed with an electric mixer until smooth. Stir in enough remaining flour to make a soft dough.

Place dough in a greased bowl; turn to grease top. Cover and let rise in a warm place (85°), free from drafts, until doubled in bulk.

Punch down dough; turn out onto a lightly floured surface. Divide dough in half; cover one portion. Roll remaining half into a 10-inch circle. Cut into 8 wedges; roll each wedge tightly, beginning at wide end. Seal points. Place rolls on a greased baking sheet, point side down; curve into crescent shapes. Repeat procedure with remaining dough.

Cover and let rise in a warm place (85°), free from drafts, 45 minutes or until doubled in bulk. Bake at 400° for 8 to 10 minutes or until lightly browned. Brush rolls with melted butter. Yield: 16 rolls.

BRAIDED WHITE BREAD

- ½ cup butter or margarine, melted
- ½ cup milk, scalded
- ½ cup sugar
- 1½ teaspoons salt
- 2 packages dry yeast
- ½ cup warm water (105° to 115°)
- 3 eggs
- 5½ to 6 cups all-purpose flour
  Melted butter or margarine (optional)

Combine ½ cup butter, milk, sugar, and salt in a large bowl; let cool to lukewarm (105° to 115°). Dissolve yeast in warm water. Stir yeast mixture into lukewarm milk mixture. Add eggs, one at a time, beating well after each addition. Add 3 cups flour; beat at medium speed with an electric mixer until smooth. Gradually stir in enough of remaining flour to make a stiff dough.

Turn out dough onto a floured surface; knead exactly 10 minutes. Cover; let rest 10 minutes.

Divide dough into 2 equal portions; cover half of dough. Roll remaining half into a 12- x 6-inch rectangle. Cut dough lengthwise into three 2-inch-wide strips, leaving a 1-inch margin at top. Braid strips; pinch loose ends to seal. Cover braid with a towel. Repeat rolling and braiding process with remaining dough. Place braids on a large greased baking sheet. Cover and let rise in a warm place (85°), free from drafts, about 1½ hours or until doubled in bulk.

Bake at 350° for 30 minutes or until braids sound hollow when tapped. Remove from pan; brush with butter, if desired. Cool on wire racks. Yield: 2 braids.

HAM AND CHEESE BRAIDS

- ½ cup water
- 1 (12-ounce) bottle beer
- 2 tablespoons sugar
- 1 teaspoon salt
- 2 tablespoons butter or margarine
- 2 cups (8 ounces) shredded Cheddar cheese
- About 5 cups all-purpose flour
- 3 packages dry yeast
- 1½ cups finely chopped, cooked ham

Combine first 6 ingredients; cook over medium heat until very warm (150°). (Cheese does not have to melt.) Set aside; cool to 120°.

Combine 2 cups flour and yeast in a large bowl; stir in warm cheese mixture. Beat at medium speed with an electric mixer 3 minutes. Stir in enough remaining flour to make a stiff dough; stir in ham.

Turn out dough onto a lightly floured surface; knead about 5 minutes, until smooth and elastic. Place in a well-greased bowl, turning to grease top. Cover and let rise in a warm place (85°), free from drafts, 50 to 60 minutes or until dough is doubled in bulk.

Grease three 9- x 5- x 3-inch loafpans, and set aside.

Punch down dough, and divide into thirds; roll each portion into a 12- x 6-inch rectangle. Cut each rectangle in thirds lengthwise; pinch ends of 3 strips together at one end to seal. Braid strips together; pinch ends to seal.

Carefully transfer braids to prepared pans. Cover and let rise in a warm place (85°), free from drafts, 40 to 50 minutes or until doubled in bulk. Bake at 350° for 30 to 35 minutes. Remove to wire racks; cool before slicing. Yield: 3 braids.

EGGNOG DOUGHNUTS

- 1 cup commercial eggnog
- ¼ cup butter or margarine
- ⅓ cup sugar
- ½ teaspoon salt
- 3⅓ cups all-purpose flour, divided
- 2 packages dry yeast
- ¾ teaspoon ground nutmeg
- 2 eggs
- Vegetable oil
- Eggnog Glaze

Combine eggnog, butter, sugar, and salt in a small saucepan; place over low heat, and cook, stirring constantly, until butter melts. Set aside, and let cool to 105° to 115°.

Combine 2 cups flour, yeast, and nutmeg; add warm eggnog mixture, and mix well. Add eggs, and beat at low speed with an electric mixer 30 seconds, scraping bowl constantly; beat at high speed an additional 3 minutes. Stir in remaining 1⅓ cups flour, mixing well. Place dough in a greased bowl, turning to grease top. Cover and chill at least 2 to 3 hours.

Punch down dough, and turn out onto a lightly floured surface. Cover and let rest 10 minutes. Roll to ⅓-inch thickness, and cut with a floured doughnut cutter. Place doughnuts several inches apart on a greased baking sheet; cover and let rise in a warm place (85°), free from drafts, about 45 to 50 minutes, until very light.

Heat 2 inches of oil in a large skillet to 375°. Add doughnuts, a few at a time, and fry 1½ to 2 minutes until golden brown on both sides, turning once. Drain well on paper towels. While still warm, dip top of each in Eggnog Glaze. Yield: about 2 dozen.

Eggnog Glaze:

- 2 cups sifted powdered sugar
- 3 tablespoons commercial eggnog
- Dash of ground nutmeg

Combine all ingredients, and mix until smooth. Yield: about 1½ cups.

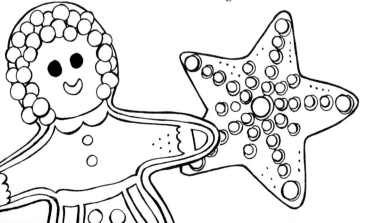

Cakes & Fruitcakes

KENTUCKY BUTTER CAKE

1 cup butter, softened
2 cups sugar
4 eggs
3 cups all-purpose flour
1 teaspoon baking powder
1 teaspoon baking soda
1 teaspoon salt
1 cup buttermilk
2 teaspoons vanilla extract
Glaze (recipe follows)
Sifted powdered sugar

Cream butter; gradually add 2 cups sugar, beating until light and fluffy. Add eggs, one at a time, beating well after each addition.

Combine dry ingredients; add to creamed mixture alternately with buttermilk, beginning and ending with flour mixture. Stir in vanilla.

Pour batter into a greased and floured 10-inch tube pan. Bake at 325° for 60 to 70 minutes or until a wooden pick inserted in center comes out clean. While cake is warm, prick surface at 1-inch intervals with a meat fork; pour glaze over cake. Let cool completely in pan. Remove from pan; sprinkle with powdered sugar just before serving. Yield: one 10-inch cake.

Glaze:

¾ cup sugar
3 tablespoons water
⅓ cup butter
2 teaspoons rum extract

Combine all ingredients in a small saucepan. Cook over medium heat, stirring constantly, until butter melts. Yield: 1¼ cups.

BROWN SUGAR POUND CAKE

1 cup butter or margarine, softened
½ cup shortening
1 (16-ounce) package light brown sugar
1 cup sugar
5 eggs
1 cup milk
1 teaspoon vanilla extract
3 cups all-purpose flour, divided
½ teaspoon salt
1 teaspoon baking powder
1⅓ cups finely chopped pecans or
    walnuts, divided
Powdered sugar glaze (recipe follows)

Cream butter and shortening; gradually add sugar, beating until light and fluffy. Add eggs, one at a time, beating well after each addition.

Combine milk and vanilla; set aside.

Combine 2¾ cups flour, salt, and baking powder; add to creamed mixture alternately with milk mixture, beginning and ending with flour mixture. Dredge 1 cup pecans in remaining ¼ cup flour; fold into batter.

Spoon batter into a greased and floured 10-inch tube pan. Bake at 350° for 1 hour and 15 minutes or until a wooden pick inserted in center comes out clean. Cool in pan 15 minutes, and remove from pan. Spoon glaze over cake, and sprinkle with remaining ⅓ cup pecans. Yield: one 10-inch cake.

Powdered Sugar Glaze:

2 tablespoons butter or margarine,
    softened
1 to 1¼ cups sifted powdered sugar
¼ cup evaporated milk

Combine all ingredients; beat at low speed with an electric mixer until smooth. Yield: enough for one 10-inch tube cake.

OLD-FASHIONED CARAMEL CAKE

⅔ cup butter or margarine, softened
1⅓ cups sugar
3 eggs
2¼ cups sifted cake flour
½ teaspoon salt
2 teaspoons baking powder
⅔ cup milk
1 teaspoon vanilla extract
Caramel Frosting
Coarsely chopped pecans (optional)
Pecan halves (optional)

Cream butter; gradually add sugar, beating until light and fluffy. Add eggs, one at a time, beating well after each addition.

Combine flour, salt, and baking powder; add to creamed mixture alternately with milk, beginning and ending with the flour mixture. Stir in the vanilla.

Pour batter into 2 greased and floured 9-inch round cakepans. Bake at 350° for 25 to 30 minutes or until a wooden pick inserted in center comes out clean. Cool layers in pans 10 minutes; remove from pans and cool completely.

Spread Caramel Frosting between layers and on top and sides of cake. Carefully press chopped pecans on sides of cake; sprinkle chopped pecans in center of cake and top with pecan halves, if desired. Yield: one 2-layer cake.

Caramel Frosting:

3 cups sugar, divided
¾ cup milk
1 egg, beaten
Pinch of salt
½ cup butter or margarine, cut into pieces

These cakes are so scrumptious, you'll be going back for seconds. Old-Fashioned Caramel Cake (top) and Toasted Butter Pecan Cake.

Sprinkle ½ cup sugar in a heavy saucepan; place over medium heat. Cook, stirring constantly, until sugar melts and syrup is light golden brown.

Combine remaining 2½ cups sugar and next 3 ingredients, mixing well; stir in butter. Stir butter mixture into hot caramelized sugar. (Mixture will tend to lump, becoming smooth with further cooking.) Cook over medium heat, stirring frequently, about 15 to 20 minutes until mixture reaches thread stage (230°). Cool 5 minutes. Beat to almost spreading consistency. Spread immediately on cooled cake. Yield: enough for one 2-layer cake.

TOASTED BUTTER PECAN CAKE

- ¼ cup butter or margarine
- 2 cups finely chopped pecans
- 1 cup butter or margarine, softened
- 2 cups sugar
- 4 eggs
- 3 cups sifted cake flour
- 2 teaspoons baking powder
- ½ teaspoon salt
- 1 cup milk
- 2 teaspoons vanilla extract
  Butter Pecan Frosting

Melt ¼ cup butter in a 13- x 9- x 2-inch baking pan. Stir in pecans, and bake at 350° for 20 minutes, stirring frequently. Set aside.

Cream 1 cup butter; gradually add sugar, beating until light and fluffy. Add eggs, one at a time, beating well after each addition.

Combine flour, baking powder, and salt; add to creamed mixture alternately with milk, beginning and ending with flour mixture. Stir in vanilla and 1⅓ cups toasted pecans, reserving remaining pecans for Butter Pecan Frosting.

Pour batter into 3 greased and floured 9-inch round cakepans. Bake at 350° for 25 to 30 minutes or until a wooden pick inserted in center comes out clean. Cool in pans 10 minutes; remove from pans, and cool completely. Spread Butter Pecan Frosting between layers and on top and sides of cake. Yield: one 3-layer cake.

Butter Pecan Frosting:

- ¼ cup plus 2 tablespoons butter or margarine, softened
- 6 cups sifted powdered sugar
- ⅓ cup evaporated milk
- 1½ teaspoons vanilla extract
  Reserved toasted pecans

Cream butter; add sugar alternately with milk, beating until light and fluffy. Stir in vanilla and reserved toasted pecans. Yield: enough for one 3-layer cake.

MAHOGANY CAKE

- 1 cup butter or margarine, softened
- 2 cups sugar
- 4 eggs
- 4 cups all-purpose flour
- 2 teaspoons baking soda
- 1½ cups buttermilk
- 1 cup chocolate syrup
- 2 teaspoons vanilla extract
  Frosting (recipe follows)

Cream butter; gradually add sugar, beating until light and fluffy. Add eggs, one at a time, beating well after each addition. Add next 5 ingredients; beat at medium speed with an electric mixer until smooth.

Pour batter into a greased 10-inch tube pan. Bake at 350° for 50 to 60 minutes or until a wooden pick inserted in center comes out clean. Cool in pan 10 minutes; remove from pan and cool completely. Spread frosting on top and sides of cake. Yield: one 10-inch cake.

Frosting:

- 2 (1-ounce) squares unsweetened chocolate
- 1 cup boiling water
- 1 cup sugar
- 3 tablespoons plus 1 teaspoon cornstarch
- ¼ teaspoon salt
- 3 tablespoons butter or margarine
- 1 teaspoon vanilla extract

Melt chocolate in boiling water in a heavy saucepan. Combine sugar, cornstarch, and salt; stir into chocolate mixture. Cook over medium heat, stirring constantly, until thickened. Remove from heat; stir in butter and vanilla. Cool to lukewarm. Yield: about 1½ cups.

GLAZED HOLIDAY CAKE

- 1 cup butter or margarine, softened
- 1 (8-ounce) package cream cheese, softened
- 1½ cups sugar
- 4 eggs
- 2¼ cups sifted cake flour, divided
- 1½ teaspoons baking powder
- 1½ teaspoons vanilla extract
- ¾ cup drained maraschino cherries
- 1 cup chopped pecans, divided
- 1½ cups sifted powdered sugar
- ¼ cup milk
  Additional maraschino cherries

Cream butter and cream cheese; gradually add 1½ cups sugar, beating until light and fluffy. Add eggs, one at a time, beating well after each addition. Combine 2 cups flour and baking powder; gradually add to creamed mixture. Stir in vanilla. Combine remaining flour, cherries, and ½ cup pecans; fold into cake batter.

Sprinkle remaining pecans into a greased 10-inch Bundt or tube pan; pour in batter. Bake at 325° for 1 hour or until a wooden pick inserted in center comes out clean. Cool 10 minutes; remove from pan, and cool completely. Combine powdered sugar and milk; spoon over cake and top with cherries. Yield: one 10-inch cake.

CLASSIC COCONUT CAKE

- 1 cup butter or margarine, softened
- 2 cups sugar
- 3 cups all-purpose flour
- 1 tablespoon baking powder
- 1 cup milk
- ½ teaspoon vanilla extract
- ½ teaspoon lemon extract
- 8 egg whites
  Pineapple Filling
  Seven-Minute Frosting
- 1¾ cups shredded coconut
  Candied red and green cherries

Cream butter; gradually add sugar, beating until light and fluffy.

Combine flour and baking powder; add to creamed mixture alternately with milk, beginning and ending with flour mixture. Stir in flavorings. Beat egg whites (at room temperature) until stiff peaks form; fold into creamed mixture.

Pour batter into 3 greased and floured 9-inch round cakepans. Bake at 350° for 25 minutes or until a wooden pick inserted in center comes out clean. Cool in pans 10 minutes; remove from pans, and cool completely. Spread Pineapple Filling between layers; spread top and sides with Seven-Minute Frosting. Sprinkle top and sides with coconut. Garnish with cherries. Yield: one 9-inch layer cake.

Pineapple Filling:

- 1 (15¼-ounce) can crushed pineapple, undrained
- 1 cup sugar
- 3 tablespoons all-purpose flour
- ¼ cup orange juice

Combine all ingredients in a medium saucepan; mix well. Cook over medium heat 15 minutes or until mixture thickens. Remove from heat, and let cool completely (mixture will be thick). Yield: about 1½ cups.

Seven-Minute Frosting:

- 1½ cups sugar
- 2 egg whites
- 1 tablespoon light corn syrup
  Dash of salt
- ⅓ cup cold water
- 1 teaspoon vanilla extract

Combine sugar, egg whites (at room temperature), corn syrup, and salt in top of a large double boiler; add cold water, and beat on low speed with an electric mixer for 30 seconds.

Place over boiling water; beat on high speed with an electric mixer 7 minutes or until stiff peaks form. Remove from heat. Add vanilla; beat 2 additional minutes or until frosting is thick. Yield: enough for one 3-layer cake.

For simple elegance, serve Classic Coconut Cake delicately garnished with candied cherries.

ORANGE CHEESECAKE

1⅔ cups graham cracker crumbs
¼ cup sugar
¼ cup butter or margarine, melted
2 (11-ounce) cans mandarin oranges, undrained
¼ cup Cointreau or Triple Sec
2½ pounds Danish cream cheese with orange, softened
1¾ cups sugar
3 tablespoons all-purpose flour
¼ teaspoon salt
¼ teaspoon vanilla extract
5 eggs
2 egg yolks
¼ cup whipping cream
½ cup orange juice
2 tablespoons cornstarch

Combine graham cracker crumbs, ¼ cup sugar, and butter; mix well. Press into bottom of a 10-inch springform pan. Bake at 375° for 8 minutes; cool.

Drain mandarin oranges, reserving ½ cup liquid. Combine mandarin oranges and Cointreau, stirring gently. Set aside, stirring occasionally.

Beat cream cheese with an electric mixer until fluffy. Stir in 1¾ cups sugar, flour, salt, and vanilla. Add eggs, one at a time, beating well after each addition; add egg yolks, and beat well. Beat in whipping cream; spread filling over crust. Bake at 400° for 8 minutes; reduce heat to 200°, and bake 1 hour and 30 minutes.

Turn off oven, and partially open oven door; leave cheesecake in oven 30 minutes. Cool on a wire rack; chill well. Remove sides from pan.

Drain mandarin oranges, reserving Cointreau. Arrange oranges on top and around sides of cheesecake.

Combine reserved mandarin orange liquid, reserved Cointreau, orange juice, and cornstarch in a saucepan; stir well. Cook over medium heat 5 minutes or until thickened; cool slightly. Spoon glaze over top of cheesecake; chill. Yield: 16 servings.

Note: The following ingredients may be substituted for Danish cream cheese with orange.

5 (8-ounce) packages cream cheese, softened
2 tablespoons finely grated orange rind
2 teaspoons orange extract

Combine all ingredients; beat with an electric mixer until fluffy.

CHRISTMAS FRUITCAKE

1 (8-ounce) package candied yellow pineapple, chopped
1 (8-ounce) package candied red cherries, chopped
1 cup raisins
¾ cup currants
2 cups chopped pecans or walnuts
½ cup white grape juice
1 cup butter or margarine, softened
2 cups firmly packed light brown sugar
5 eggs
1 teaspoon almond extract
2¼ cups all-purpose flour
¼ teaspoon baking soda
½ teaspoon ground cinnamon
½ teaspoon ground mace
Brandy

Grease a 10-inch tube pan; line with waxed paper and grease well. Set aside.

Combine first 5 ingredients; add grape juice, mixing well. Let stand 1 hour.

Cream butter; gradually add sugar, beating until light and fluffy. Add eggs, one at a time, beating well after each addition.

Combine dry ingredients; gradually add to creamed mixture, and mix well. Add flavoring and stir in fruit. Spoon into prepared pan. Bake at 275° for 3 hours and 20 minutes or until cake tests done. Cool cake in pan 30 minutes. Remove from pan, peel paper liner from cake, and cool completely. Wrap in brandy-soaked cheesecloth and store in an airtight container for 1 week. Store in refrigerator. Yield: one 10-inch cake.

Confections

DOUBLE ALMOND TOFFEE

    2 cups butter or margarine
 2½ cups sugar
 1½ cups whole unblanched almonds
 1½ cups semisweet chocolate morsels,
        melted
 1½ cups chopped almonds, lightly toasted

Melt butter in a large, heavy skillet; add sugar. Cook, stirring constantly, over high heat about 6 minutes until mixture foams vigorously. Reduce heat to low; cook, stirring constantly, 5 minutes.

Add whole almonds to sugar mixture; increase heat to high. Cook, stirring constantly, about 5 minutes, until almonds begin to pop.

Reduce heat; cook, stirring constantly, 7 minutes. (If mixture begins to turn dark brown, remove from heat but continue to stir entire 7 minutes.) Pour into a 15- x 10- x 1-inch pan; cool until firm.

Spread half of melted chocolate over toffee layer. Sprinkle with half of chopped almonds; cool. (Refrigerate if necessary to firm chocolate.)

Turn out candy onto waxed paper; spread remaining chocolate over other side. Sprinkle with remaining chopped almonds; cool. Break into pieces. Store in waxed paper-lined, covered metal containers. Yield: about 3 pounds.

ROCKY ROAD CLUSTERS

    9 (1-ounce) squares semisweet
        chocolate
 ½ cup chopped salted peanuts
 ½ cup creamy peanut butter
    1 cup miniature marshmallows
 ¼ cup shredded coconut

Place chocolate in top of a double boiler; bring water to a boil. Reduce heat to low; cook until chocolate melts, stirring occasionally.

Combine remaining ingredients in large bowl; add chocolate, mixing well. Drop by rounded tablespoonfuls onto waxed paper; chill until firm. Store in covered container in refrigerator. Yield: about 1½ dozen.

CHRISTMAS HARD CANDY

        Butter or margarine
    1 cup sifted powdered sugar
    2 cups sugar
    1 cup water
 ¾ cup light corn syrup
 ¾ teaspoon oil of cinnamon
    3 to 5 drops red food coloring

Assemble the following equipment before starting recipe: marble slab, large bowl, wooden spoon, and scissors. A partner may be helpful.

Grease marble slab with butter; set aside. Pour 1 cup powdered sugar into a large bowl.

Combine 2 cups sugar, water, and corn syrup in a Dutch oven; cook over medium heat, without stirring, until mixture reaches hard crack stage (300°). Remove from heat; stir in oil of cinnamon and food coloring.

Pour hot sugar mixture onto prepared marble slab; work mixture quickly towards center with wooden spoon 2 to 3 minutes or until mixture thickens. Quickly cut long strips from candy with scissors; cut each strip into 1-inch pieces, letting candy fall directly into powdered sugar. Remove candy from powdered sugar, and store at room temperature. Yield: 7½ dozen.

Note: Oil of cinnamon may be purchased at drug stores.

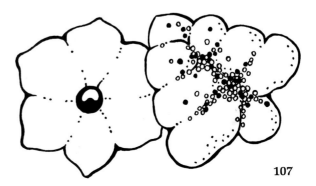

FRENCH CREMES

2 cups sugar
1 cup whipping cream
1 tablespoon light corn syrup
⅛ teaspoon salt
½ teaspoon cold water
Yellow, green, and red food coloring
¼ teaspoon lemon extract
¼ teaspoon imitation butter flavoring
¼ teaspoon peppermint extract
Pecan halves

Combine first 4 ingredients in a large Dutch oven; cook over medium heat, stirring occasionally, until mixture reaches soft ball stage (234°). Sprinkle a 13- x 9- x 2-inch baking pan with ½ teaspoon cold water; carefully pour hot mixture into pan, and let cool, without stirring, to lukewarm (110°). Work mixture gently towards center with a wooden spoon until smooth and creamy.

Divide candy into 3 equal portions. Add 2 drops yellow food coloring and lemon extract to 1 portion; knead until color is evenly distributed. Add 2 drops green food coloring and butter flavoring to second portion; repeat kneading procedure. Add 2 drops red food coloring and peppermint extract to remaining portion; repeat kneading procedure.

Shape candy into 1-inch balls; place a pecan half on top of each, and press gently to flatten. Store in an airtight container in refrigerator. Yield: about 2 dozen.

Candy lovers will be delighted with these irresistible confections. Top candy tier: Mocha-Bourbon Balls and Holiday Divinity; lower tier: French Crèmes; then clockwise: Christmas Hard Candy, Mocha-Bourbon Balls, French Crèmes, and Rocky Road Clusters.

MOCHA-BOURBON BALLS

12 (1-ounce) squares semisweet chocolate
½ cup butter
⅓ cup sugar
½ cup whipping cream
¼ cup bourbon
1 tablespoon instant coffee granules
2 cups ground pecans, divided
¾ cup chocolate wafer crumbs

Combine chocolate, butter, and sugar in top of a double boiler; bring water to a boil. Reduce heat to low; cook until chocolate and butter melt. Remove from heat; stir in cream, bourbon, coffee granules, and 1 cup pecans. Cover and refrigerate until firm.

Combine remaining pecans and wafer crumbs; mix well. Shape chocolate mixture into 1-inch balls and roll in crumb mixture. Store in refrigerator. Yield: about 5 dozen.

HOLIDAY DIVINITY

3 cups sugar
1 cup light corn syrup
½ cup water
¼ teaspoon salt
2 egg whites
1 teaspoon vanilla extract
1 cup finely chopped pecans

Combine first 4 ingredients in a Dutch oven; cook over low heat, stirring constantly, until sugar dissolves. Increase heat to high, and cook, without stirring, until mixture reaches hard ball stage (260°).

Beat egg whites (at room temperature) in a large mixing bowl until stiff peaks form. Pour hot sugar mixture in a thin stream over egg whites while beating constantly at high speed with an electric mixer. Add vanilla, and continue beating 5 to 10 minutes, until mixture holds its shape. Stir in pecans. Drop by teaspoonfuls onto waxed paper. Yield: about 3½ dozen.

NUTTY MARSHMALLOW LOG

2 cups chopped pecans
About 1¼ cups sifted powdered sugar, divided
1 (16-ounce) package marshmallows
3 to 4 tablespoons peanut butter

Combine pecans and 1 cup powdered sugar; sprinkle evenly over a large sheet of waxed paper, and set aside.

Place marshmallows in top of a double boiler; bring water to a boil. Reduce heat to low; cook until marshmallows melt. Stir in peanut butter. Pour marshmallow mixture over powdered sugar-pecan mixture. Mix with hands until pecans and sugar are blended into marshmallow mixture and mixture resembles soft dough.

Shape into 2 rolls, 1 inch in diameter. Let stand about 45 minutes. Roll candy in remaining powdered sugar. Let stand at least 30 minutes. Cut into ¼-inch slices. Store in a covered container, separating layers with waxed paper. Yield: about 100 slices.

CHOCOLATE-NUT CRUNCH

½ cup chopped pecans
¾ cup firmly packed brown sugar
½ cup butter
1 (6-ounce) package semisweet chocolate morsels

Sprinkle pecans in a lightly greased 9-inch square baking pan, leaving a 1-inch margin from edges of pan.

Combine sugar and butter in a small saucepan; cook over low heat, stirring constantly, until mixtures reaches a boil. Boil 4 minutes, stirring constantly. Remove from heat; pour over pecans in pan.

Sprinkle chocolate morsels over top of butter mixture; cover with foil and let stand 2 minutes. Remove foil and spread melted morsels evenly over top. Chill at least 3 hours or until firm. Break candy into serving pieces; store in refrigerator. Yield: 6 to 8 servings.

COCONUT CARAMELS

1 cup sugar
¾ cup light corn syrup
1½ cups half-and-half, divided
1 (3½-ounce) can flaked coconut
2 tablespoons butter or margarine
1 tablespoon vanilla extract

Combine sugar, corn syrup, and ½ cup half-and-half in a heavy saucepan. Cook over low heat, stirring constantly, until mixture reaches thread stage (230°).

Add ½ cup half-and-half; cook, stirring constantly, until mixture reaches thread stage (230°). Add remaining ½ cup half-and-half; cook, stirring constantly, until mixture again reaches thread stage (230°).

Remove mixture from heat; add coconut, butter, and vanilla. Stir until butter melts. Pour into a greased 8- x 4- x 3-inch loafpan; cool.

Turn out candy onto a marble slab or waxed paper. Cut into 1-inch squares. Let stand overnight. Wrap individually in plastic wrap. Yield: about 32 (1-inch) pieces.

SOUTHERN PRALINES

2 cups sugar
½ cup milk
½ cup light corn syrup
2 tablespoons butter or margarine
¼ teaspoon baking soda
1 teaspoon vanilla extract
2 cups pecans

Combine first 5 ingredients in a heavy saucepan; mix well. Cook over medium heat, stirring until sugar dissolves; cook until mixture reaches soft ball stage (232°). Remove from heat; add vanilla and beat until creamy. Stir in pecans. Drop from a spoon onto waxed paper; let stand until firm. Yield: 3 dozen.

Gift Ideas

CAFE AU LAIT MIX

½ cup nondairy coffee creamer
½ cup sugar
⅓ cup instant coffee powder

Combine ingredients in a small mixing bowl, blending well. To serve, place 1 tablespoon mix in a cup. Add 4 ounces boiling water, and stir well. Store mix in an airtight container. Yield: enough mix for twenty 4-ounce servings.

Café Viennese:

1 tablespoon Café au Lait Mix
1 tablespoon Cognac
Dash of ground nutmeg

Place ingredients in a cup. Add 4 ounces boiling water. Stir well. Yield: one 4-ounce serving.

Café Mexicano:

1 tablespoon Café au Lait Mix
1 tablespoon Kahlúa or other
   coffee-flavored liqueur
Dash of ground cinnamon
1 teaspoon grated semisweet chocolate

Place ingredients in a cup. Add 4 ounces boiling water. Stir well. Yield: one 4-ounce serving.

Mocha Java:

1 tablespoon Café au Lait Mix
1 tablespoon crème de cacao
1¼ teaspoons hot cocoa mix or instant
   chocolate malt mix

Place ingredients in a cup. Add 4 ounces boiling water. Stir well. Yield: one 4-ounce serving.

NINE BEAN SOUP MIX

1 pound barley pearls
1 pound dried black beans
1 pound dried red beans
1 pound dried pinto beans
1 pound dried navy beans
1 pound dried Great Northern beans
1 pound dried lentils
1 pound dried split peas
1 pound dried black-eyed peas

Combine all beans. Divide into ten 2-cup packages for gift giving, and present with the following recipe for Nine Bean Soup. Prepare mix according to Nine Bean Soup recipe. Yield: ten 2-cup packages.

NINE BEAN SOUP

2 cups Nine Bean Soup Mix
2 quarts water
1 pound ham, diced
1 large onion, chopped
1 clove garlic, minced
½ to ¾ teaspoon salt
1 (16-ounce) can tomatoes, undrained
   and chopped
1 (10-ounce) can tomatoes and green
   chiles, undrained

Sort and wash 2 cups bean mix; place in a Dutch oven. Cover with water 2 inches above beans, and soak overnight. Drain beans; add 2 quarts water and next 4 ingredients. Cover and bring to a boil; reduce heat, and simmer 1½ hours or until beans are tender. Add remaining ingredients; simmer 30 minutes, stirring occasionally. Yield: 8 cups.

GLAZED LEMON-NUT BREAD

¼ cup butter or margarine, softened
¾ cup sugar
2 eggs
2 cups all-purpose flour
2½ teaspoons baking powder
1 teaspoon salt
¾ cup milk ½ + ½
2 teaspoons grated lemon rind
½ cup finely chopped walnuts
¼ cup plus 1 tablespoon sifted powdered
   sugar
1 teaspoon lemon juice

Cream butter; gradually add ¾ cup sugar, beating until light and fluffy. Add eggs, one at a time, beating well after each addition.

Combine flour, baking powder, and salt; add to creamed mixture alternately with milk, beginning and ending with flour mixture. Stir in lemon rind and walnuts.

Pour batter into a greased 9- x 5- x 3-inch loafpan. Bake at 350° for 45 to 50 minutes. Cool in pan 10 minutes; remove to a wire rack, and let cool completely.

Combine powdered sugar and lemon juice; stir until smooth. Drizzle glaze over top of bread. Yield: 1 loaf.

ORANGE-LEMON MARMALADE

3 cups thinly sliced orange rind
3½ cups chopped orange pulp
3½ cups thinly sliced lemon
1½ quarts water
   About 5½ cups sugar

Combine fruit and 1½ quarts water in a large Dutch oven; place over medium heat, and simmer 5 minutes. Cover, and let mixture stand 12 to 18 hours in a cool place.

Bring mixture to a boil; reduce heat to medium, and cook 45 minutes or until rind is tender. Measure fruit mixture, including liquid; add 1 cup sugar per 1 cup fruit mixture. Bring to a slow boil, stirring until sugar dissolves. Cook rapidly about 15 minutes, stirring frequently as mixture thickens.

Pour marmalade into hot sterilized jars, leaving ¼-inch headspace; cover at once with metal lids, and screw bands tight. Process jars 10 minutes in a boiling-water bath. Yield: 7 half-pints.

NUTTY POPCORN BALLS

2 cups sugar
¾ cup light corn syrup
¾ cup water
1½ teaspoons salt
½ cup butter or margarine
1½ teaspoons vanilla extract
3 quarts popped corn
1 cup coarsely chopped pecans

Combine sugar, corn syrup, water, and salt in a heavy saucepan; cook over medium heat, stirring until sugar dissolves. Cook, without stirring, until syrup reaches hard ball stage (250°). Remove from heat, and stir in butter and vanilla.

Combine popped corn and pecans in large pan; pour hot syrup over top, mixing well. Grease hands with butter, and shape mixture into balls; place on waxed paper to dry. Yield: about 1 dozen.

Make gifts in your kitchen; choose from this array of goodies especially suited for gift giving. From back left: Sugared Peanuts, Tart Garlic Marinade, Nine Bean Soup Mix, Orange-Lemon Marmalade, and Zesty Salad Dressing. Front: Glazed Lemon-Nut Bread, Seasoned Salt, and Nutty Popcorn Balls.

SUGARED PEANUTS

2 cups raw, blanched peanuts
1 cup sugar
½ cup water
½ teaspoon salt, divided

Combine peanuts, sugar, and water in a heavy saucepan; cook over medium heat, stirring constantly for 10 to 15 minutes, until sugar is crystallized and coats each peanut.

Spoon mixture onto a lightly greased cookie sheet; sprinkle with ¼ teaspoon salt. Bake at 300° for 10 minutes. Remove from oven and sprinkle with remaining ¼ teaspoon salt. Return to oven and continue to bake at 300° for 10 minutes. Cool and store in an airtight container. Yield: 2 cups.

ORANGE ALMONDS

1½ cups whole blanched almonds, lightly toasted
1 egg white, slightly beaten
¾ cup sifted powdered sugar
1½ teaspoons grated orange rind
Dash of ground nutmeg

Combine almonds and egg white; set aside. Combine remaining ingredients. Drain almonds, and stir into sugar mixture until well coated. Spread onto a greased baking sheet. Bake at 250° for 20 to 30 minutes or until coating is dry and almonds are crisp; stir almonds occasionally. Yield: 1½ cups.

SEASONED SALT

¼ cup plus 2 tablespoons salt
2¼ teaspoons paprika
1 teaspoon dry mustard
½ teaspoon garlic salt
½ teaspoon celery salt
½ teaspoon curry powder
½ teaspoon dried whole thyme
½ teaspoon dried whole marjoram
¼ teaspoon onion powder
⅛ teaspoon dillseeds

Combine all ingredients in a small jar; cover and shake mixture until well blended. Store in an airtight container. Yield: about ½ cup.

ZESTY SALAD DRESSING

1½ cups vegetable oil
1 cup tomato soup, undiluted
¾ cup sugar
⅔ cup vinegar
2 tablespoons dried whole oregano
2 teaspoons dry mustard
1 teaspoon onion powder
1 teaspoon garlic salt
½ teaspoon salt
½ teaspoon paprika

Combine all ingredients in container of electric blender; process until smooth. Chill. Yield: 4 cups.

TART GARLIC MARINADE

¾ cup vinegar
¾ cup vegetable oil
½ to ¾ cup soy sauce
¼ cup hot sauce
¼ to ½ cup Worcestershire sauce
½ cup vermouth
¼ cup honey
¼ cup wine vinegar
5 cloves garlic, crushed
1½ teaspoons dry mustard
1 tablespoon salt
¾ teaspoon cracked black peppercorns

Combine all ingredients in a saucepan, and simmer 10 minutes. Store in refrigerator until ready to use. Use marinade with steak or poultry. Yield: about 4 cups.

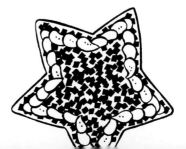

Party Fare

CHERRY-CREAM CROWN

2 (3-ounce) packages ladyfingers
¼ cup brandy or rum
1 (8-ounce) package cream cheese, softened
½ cup sugar
1 pint whipping cream, whipped
1 teaspoon vanilla extract
1 (21-ounce) can cherry pie filling

Split ladyfingers lengthwise; brush lightly with brandy or rum. Line sides of a 9-inch springform pan with half of the ladyfingers; set aside.

Beat cream cheese and sugar until smooth and creamy; gently fold in whipped cream and vanilla. Spread one-third of cream cheese mixture in bottom of prepared pan, and top with half of remaining ladyfingers; repeat layers. Top with remaining cream cheese mixture. Cover and chill at least 8 hours.

Spread pie filling over cheese layer; chill 2 to 3 hours. Remove sides from pan and serve. Yield: 12 to 14 servings.

GRAND MARNIER PUFFS

1 cup water
½ cup butter or margarine
¼ teaspoon salt
1 cup all-purpose flour
4 eggs
Crème Pâtissière
Sifted powdered sugar
Orange and lemon slices (optional)

Combine water, butter, and salt in a saucepan; bring to a boil. Add flour all at once, stirring vigorously; cook over low heat for approximately 1 minute or until mixture leaves sides of pan and forms a smooth ball. Remove from heat and allow to cool slightly.

Add eggs, one at a time, beating with a wooden spoon after each addition; beat until batter is smooth. Drop rounded teaspoonfuls of batter 2 inches apart on a greased baking sheet.

Bake at 425° for 15 minutes. Reduce temperature to 350°, and bake an additional 8 minutes. (Inside should be dry and firm.) Cool away from drafts. Cut tops off puffs; pull out and discard any soft dough inside.

Fill bottom of each puff with Crème Pâtissière. Replace tops, and sprinkle with powdered sugar. Garnish with orange and lemon slices, if desired. Yield: about 3 dozen.

Crème Pâtissière:

¾ cup sugar
7 egg yolks
⅓ cup all-purpose flour
Pinch of salt
2 cups milk, scalded
1½ teaspoons vanilla extract
Grated rind of 3 oranges
1 to 2 tablespoons Grand Marnier or other orange-flavored liqueur

Combine sugar and egg yolks, beating until light and lemon colored. Combine flour and salt; gradually add to yolk mixture, beating well. Gradually stir milk into yolk mixture; pour into a heavy saucepan. Cook over low heat until thickened, stirring constantly.

Remove custard from heat; stir in vanilla, orange rind, and Grand Marnier. Cover with plastic wrap, pressing wrap onto surface to prevent formation of film. Chill well. Yield: about 3 cups.

115

SMOKED EGG DIP

12 hard-cooked eggs, finely chopped
2 tablespoons butter or margarine,
    softened
1 tablespoon lemon juice or vinegar
2 teaspoons prepared mustard
2 teaspoons Worcestershire sauce
1½ teaspoons liquid smoke
8 drops of hot sauce
¾ teaspoon salt
½ teaspoon pepper
1 cup mayonnaise
1 thinly sliced radish

Combine all ingredients except radish; beat at medium speed with an electric mixer until smooth. Chill at least 1 hour; beat until fluffy.

Garnish with radish slices; serve with fresh vegetables. Yield: about 4 cups.

CHEESIES

1 egg white, slightly beaten
1 teaspoon water
1½ cups (6 ounces) shredded Swiss
    cheese
¼ cup grated Parmesan cheese
½ cup butter or margarine, softened
¾ cup all-purpose flour
¾ teaspoon salt
⅛ teaspoon ground nutmeg
Paprika (optional)

Combine egg white and water, beating lightly with a fork; set aside.

Combine cheese and butter, mixing well. Add flour, salt, and nutmeg; stir with a fork until a stiff dough is formed. Cover and chill 15 minutes.

Shape dough into ¾-inch balls, and place on a greased baking sheet. Flatten each with a fork, and brush with egg white mixture.

Bake at 425° for 10 minutes or just until the edges begin to brown. Allow to cool, and sprinkle tops lightly with paprika, if desired. Yield: about 3 dozen.

Let your holiday guests feast on these delicious appetizers. Clockwise: Fried Wontons, Smoked Egg Dip, Cheesies, and Shrimp-Vegetable Marinade.

SHRIMP-VEGETABLE MARINADE

3 pounds large shrimp, cooked, peeled,
    and deveined
2 (8½-ounce) cans artichoke hearts,
    drained
½ pound fresh mushrooms, halved
1 pint cherry tomatoes
    Tarragon Marinade
    Leaf lettuce (optional)

Combine shrimp, artichoke hearts, mushrooms, and tomatoes in an airtight plastic container; add Tarragon Marinade. Cover tightly and chill 18 to 24 hours. Drain before serving.

Spoon shrimp mixture over lettuce, if desired. Yield: 24 to 30 appetizer servings.

Tarragon Marinade:

¾ cup tarragon vinegar
1 small onion, quartered
1 tablespoon crushed garlic
1½ teaspoons lemon juice
½ teaspoon brown sugar
½ teaspoon salad herbs
⅛ teaspoon prepared mustard
¼ teaspoon salt
¼ teaspoon pepper
2 cups vegetable oil
½ cup olive oil

Combine all ingredients except vegetable oil and olive oil in container of electric blender; blend at medium speed about 5 seconds. Add oil, stirring until blended. Yield: about 3¼ cups.

117

FRIED WONTONS

- 1 **pound ground pork**
- 2 **green onions, finely chopped**
- 1 **(8½-ounce) can water chestnuts, drained and finely chopped**
- 1 **stalk celery, finely chopped**
- 2 **eggs, beaten**
- 1 **tablespoon soy sauce**
- 1 **teaspoon salt**
- ½ **teaspoon pepper**
- 1 **(16-ounce) package wonton skins**
  Vegetable oil
  Commercial sweet-and-sour sauce (optional)

Cook ground pork until browned, stirring to crumble. Drain off pan drippings. Stir in next 7 ingredients.

Place 1 teaspoon of pork mixture in center of each wonton skin. Tuck top corner over and under the filling, rolling until tight. Lightly brush left and right corners of wonton with water. Holding center back of wonton with your middle finger, fold left and right corners back around your fingers. Overlap left and right corners and press so they adhere, letting remaining corner flap loosely.

Heat 2 inches of vegetable oil to 375° in wok or large skillet. Add 6 wontons at a time, and fry 30 seconds on each side until golden brown. Drain well on paper towels. Repeat with remaining wontons. Serve hot with sweet-and-sour sauce, if desired. Yield: 40 to 50.

ITALIAN MEATBALL NIBBLES

- 1 **pound lean ground beef**
- ¼ **cup commercial seasoned breadcrumbs**
- ¼ **cup grated Romano cheese**
- ½ **teaspoon chopped fresh or dried mint**
- ⅛ **teaspoon pepper**
- ⅛ **teaspoon salt**
- 1 **clove garlic, crushed**
  Grated Parmesan cheese

Combine all ingredients except Parmesan cheese; mix well. Form mixture into 1-inch balls, and place in a lightly greased baking pan. Bake at 350° for 20 to 25 minutes or until done, turning occasionally. Roll each meatball in Parmesan cheese. Serve warm. Yield: about 2½ dozen.

MEXI-CHILE DIP

- 1 **(4-ounce) can green chiles, drained and chopped**
- 1 **(3-ounce) can pitted black olives, drained and chopped**
- 1 **medium onion, chopped**
- 1 **large tomato, chopped**
- 3 **tablespoons olive oil**
- 1½ **tablespoons vinegar**
- 1 **teaspoon garlic salt**

Combine first 4 ingredients in a small bowl. Combine remaining ingredients, and add to vegetable mixture. Chill at least 2 hours before serving. Serve with corn chips. Yield: 2½ cups.

GREAT GUACAMOLE

- 4 **avocados, peeled and chopped**
- 2 **tomatoes, chopped**
- ¼ **cup chopped onion**
- 1 to 1½ **teaspoons salt**
- 1 **tablespoon mayonnaise**
- 1 **teaspoon lemon juice**
- ¼ **teaspoon hot sauce**

Combine all ingredients in container of an electric blender; process until smooth. Chill. Serve with corn chips. Yield: about 3 cups.

Pies

OLD-FASHIONED EGG CUSTARD PIE

    3 eggs, beaten
    ¾ cup sugar
    ¼ teaspoon salt
    1 teaspoon vanilla extract
    ½ teaspoon ground nutmeg
    2 cups milk, scalded
    1 unbaked 9-inch pastry shell
       Ground nutmeg

Combine eggs and sugar, beating well; add salt, vanilla, and ½ teaspoon nutmeg. Gradually add scalded milk, stirring constantly. Pour mixture into pastry shell, and sprinkle top with additional nutmeg.

Bake at 400° for 10 minutes. Reduce oven temperature to 325°, and bake an additional 25 minutes or until a knife inserted halfway between center and edge comes out clean. Cool thoroughly before serving. Yield: one 9-inch pie.

FRENCH SILK PIE

    ½ cup butter or margarine, softened
    ¾ cup sugar
    1 (1-ounce) square unsweetened
         chocolate, melted
    2 eggs
    1 teaspoon vanilla extract
    1 baked 8-inch pastry shell
       Whipped cream
       Chocolate shavings or chopped
         pecans

Cream butter; gradually add sugar, beating until light and fluffy. Stir in melted chocolate. Add eggs, one at a time, beating with an electric mixer for 5 minutes after each addition or until sugar is completely dissolved. Stir in vanilla.

Pour into baked pastry shell; top with whipped cream, and sprinkle with chocolate shavings or pecans. Chill. Yield: one 8-inch pie.

ICE CREAM PIE SPECTACULAR

    1 cup graham cracker crumbs
    ½ cup chopped walnuts
    ¼ cup butter or margarine, melted
    1 pint coffee ice cream, softened
    1 pint vanilla ice cream, softened
       Brown Sugar Sauce

Combine graham cracker crumbs, walnuts, and butter; mix well. Press mixture firmly into a buttered 9-inch pieplate. Bake at 375° for 8 to 10 minutes; cool.

Spread coffee ice cream evenly over crust; freeze. Spread vanilla ice cream over coffee ice cream layer; cover and freeze until firm. To serve, cut into slices and top with warm Brown Sugar Sauce. Yield: one 9-inch pie.

Brown Sugar Sauce:

    3 tablespoons butter or margarine
    1 cup firmly packed brown sugar
    ½ cup half-and-half
    1 cup chopped walnuts
    1 teaspoon vanilla extract

Melt butter in a heavy saucepan over low heat; stir in brown sugar. Cook 5 to 8 minutes, stirring constantly. Remove from heat, and gradually stir in half-and-half. Cook 1 minute, and remove from heat. Stir in walnuts and vanilla. Yield: about 1½ cups.

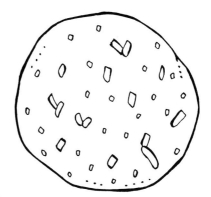

SOUTHERN PECAN PIE

½ cup butter or margarine
1 cup sugar
1 cup light corn syrup
4 eggs, beaten
1 teaspoon vanilla extract
¼ teaspoon salt
1 unbaked 9-inch pastry shell
1 cup pecan halves

Combine butter, sugar, and corn syrup; cook over low heat, stirring constantly, until sugar is dissolved. Cool. Add eggs, vanilla, and salt; mix well. Pour filling into pastry shell, and top with pecan halves. Bake at 325° for 50 to 55 minutes. Yield: one 9-inch pie.

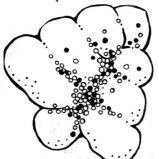

SWEET POTATO PIE

3 cups cooked, mashed sweet potatoes
2 tablespoons butter or margarine, softened
2 cups sugar
1 teaspoon baking soda
1 teaspoon baking powder
1 teaspoon ground cinnamon
¼ teaspoon ground cloves
¼ teaspoon ground allspice
¼ teaspoon ground nutmeg
1 cup buttermilk
3 eggs, slightly beaten
1 teaspoon vanilla extract
2 unbaked 9-inch pastry shells
Whipped cream (optional)
Coarsely chopped pecans (optional)

Combine first 9 ingredients; beat at medium speed with an electric mixer until smooth. Stir in buttermilk, eggs, and vanilla.

Pour sweet potato mixture into pastry shells. Bake at 400° for 10 minutes; reduce heat to 350° and bake 35 minutes. (Place foil on edges if pastry is browning too much.) Cool completely. Garnish pies with whipped cream and pecans, if desired. Yield: two 9-inch pies.

FESTIVE CRANBERRY PIE

¾ cup sugar
1 tablespoon cornstarch
¾ cup light corn syrup
½ cup water
2 tablespoons grated orange rind
½ cup raisins
½ cup coarsely chopped pecans
3 cups fresh cranberries
2 tablespoons butter or margarine
Pastry for double-crust 9-inch pie
2 teaspoons sugar

Combine first 5 ingredients in a large saucepan, mixing well; bring to a boil. Stir in raisins, pecans, and cranberries. Cover, reduce heat, and cook 7 to 10 minutes or until cranberry skins pop. Remove from heat and stir in butter; cool completely without stirring.

Roll half of pastry to ⅛-inch thickness on a lightly floured surface; fit into a 9-inch pieplate. Spoon filling into pastry shell. Roll remaining pastry to ¼-inch thickness; cut into 1-inch strips. Weave strips over filling in a lattice fashion, twisting each strip while weaving. Press ends of strips into rim of crust; flute edge. Sprinkle pie with sugar. Bake at 400° for 40 minutes. Yield: one 9-inch pie.

Slice a piece of holiday tradition with (top to bottom) Southern Pecan Pie, Sweet Potato Pie, and Festive Cranberry Pie.

APRICOT SOUFFLE PIE

1 (6-ounce) package dried apricots
3 eggs
1¼ to 1½ cups sugar
¼ cup water
1 (8-ounce) carton commercial sour
   cream
1½ teaspoons vanilla extract
1 unbaked 9-inch pastry shell

Soak apricots in water to cover 1 hour; drain and set aside. Place eggs in container of electric blender; process on medium speed 10 seconds. Add sugar and blend 30 seconds longer. Add apricots, ¼ cup water, sour cream, and vanilla; process 20 seconds. Pour mixture into pastry shell, and bake at 375° for 45 minutes or until the center of pie is firm. Yield: one 9-inch pie.

PRALINE APPLE PIE

1 unbaked 9-inch pastry shell
6 cups peeled, thinly sliced cooking
   apples
¾ cup sugar
¼ cup plus 2 tablespoons all-purpose
   flour
½ teaspoon ground mace
¼ teaspoon salt
2 tablespoons butter or margarine
1 tablespoon lemon juice
¼ cup butter or margarine
½ cup firmly packed brown sugar
2 tablespoons whipping cream
½ cup coarsely chopped pecans

Prick bottom and sides of pastry shell with a fork. Bake at 400° for 5 minutes; set aside.

Combine apples, sugar, flour, mace, and salt. Toss gently. Spoon into pastry shell; dot with 2 tablespoons butter and sprinkle with lemon

juice. Bake at 400° for 45 minutes. (Place foil on edges if pastry is browning too much.) Remove from oven.

Melt ¼ cup butter in a small saucepan; stir in brown sugar and whipping cream. Cook over low heat, stirring constantly, just to boiling. Stir in pecans and pour over top of pie. Return to oven for 5 minutes or until topping bubbles. Yield: one 9-inch pie.

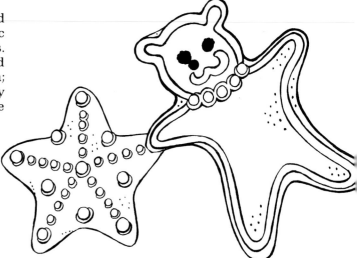

BAKED ALASKA MINCEMEAT PIE

1 (9-ounce) package dry mincemeat or
   1½ cups prepared mincemeat
1 quart vanilla ice cream, softened
1 baked 9-inch pastry shell
3 egg whites
¼ cup plus 2 tablespoons sugar

Boil dry mincemeat in ½ cup water 3 minutes; cool (do not drain). If prepared mincemeat is used, heat thoroughly and then cool.

Combine mincemeat and ice cream; spoon into pastry shell. Freeze until firm.

Beat egg whites (at room temperature) until foamy. Gradually add sugar, 1 tablespoon at a time, beating until stiff peaks form. (Meringue should be light and dry.) Spread over frozen pie, and bake at 450° for 3 to 4 minutes or until lightly browned. Serve immediately. Yield: 8 servings.

Christmas Journal

Santa has been keeping lists for years, and we all know how jolly he is when it is time for him to pop down the chimney to leave the gifts. While Santa is making his list and checking it twice, each of us must also be making plans. There are gifts to buy, parties to plan and more to attend, friends to call, cards to send, cookies to bake—and all the other things that make up this joyously busy season.

"Christmas Journal" has a place for all your lists. A card list will help you remember to whom you want to send cards; checking off the names will let you know just how far you have gotten with addressing and mailing. Size charts make gift buying easier for everyone because sizes are handy and there is no need to try to ask the size without identifying the gift. Another section is designed for gifts and wishes. Use these lists as a gift list or as a place for the family to write in very big hints about the gifts they would like to have.

A Holiday Calendar will help you schedule the events of the season. Ask everyone in the family to help you keep the calendar up to date, so you know when you have parties and when cupcakes must be made for the school fair.

Mailing

CARDS

As you are planning your Christmas cards, keep in mind the following regulations by the U.S. Postal Service. All envelopes must be rectangular in shape. Cards and envelopes smaller than 3½" × 5" cannot be mailed. Envelopes larger than 6⅛" × 11½", even if they weigh less than 1 ounce, require extra postage.

PACKAGES

Packages may be sent through the U.S. Postal Service by parcel post in weights up to 40 pounds (70 pounds for rural routes and small towns) and measurements of 84" of combined length and girth. "Priority" and "Express Mail" (at higher prices) can be used for packages up to 70 pounds in weight and up to 100" in combined length and girth. Refer to the chart for requirements of packaging, closing, and addressing.

United Parcel Service (UPS) accepts packages up to 50 pounds and up to 108" in combined length and girth. There is a pick-up fee for door-to-door service, but in peak periods, you may find it more convenient to take the package to UPS customer service.

CATEGORY	EXAMPLES	CONTAINER	CUSHIONING	CLOSURE
Soft Goods		Self-supporting box or tear-resistant bag		Reinforced tape or sealed bag
Liquids		Leak proof interior and secondary containers	Absorbent	Sealed with filament tape
Powders		Must be sift-proof		Sealed with filament tape
Perishables		Impermeable to content odor	Absorbent	Sealed with filament tape
Fragile Items		Fiberboard (minimum 175 lb test)	To distribute shocks and separate from container surfaces with foamed plastic or padding	Sealed and reinforced with filament tape
Awkward Loads		Fiberboard tubes and boxes with length not over 10 times girth	Pre-formed fiberboard or foamed plastic shapes	Tube ends equal to side wall strength

CONTAINER	CUSHIONING	CLOSURE	ADDRESSING
Fiberboard Manufacturer's Certificate 125 lb test to 20 lbs 175 lb test to 40 lbs 275 lb test to 70 lbs Paperboard up to 10 lbs	Wrap each item individually with enough padding to prevent damage from shock Separate wrapped items from outer package surfaces with padding or foamed plastic	Pressure Sensitive Filament Tape is preferable to prevent accidental opening Reinforced Kraft Paper Tape Kraft Paper Tape	Address Labels should be readable from 30" away and should not be easily smeared or washed off Should contain ZIP Code Return Address should also be included inside of carton

Adapted from a U.S. Postal Service poster.

Christmas Card List

Name	rec'd	sent

Name	rec'd	sent

CHRISTMAS CARD LIST (CONTINUED)

Name	rec'd	sent

Name	rec'd	sent

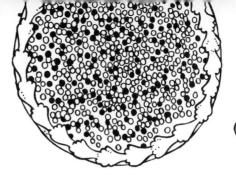

CHRISTMAS CARD LIST (CONTINUED)

Name	rec'd	sent

Name	rec'd	sent

Gifts & Wishes

Name

Mom Callahan -
diamond   full   calico
ear blobs   apron,

Kathy -

Name

Children:

Jesse
Coles
Kate

Melissa

Name

whats its step Callahan

Name

Name

Name

Betty Hean

Name

Harry Hean
Barbie   "

Catty   "

Name

Aunt Bart -
Gus -

Name

Name

Name

Name

128

Size Charts

Name			
Name			
Name			
Name			
Name			
Name			
Name			

Name _Hank_		Name _Mimi_	
height _5-11½_	weight	height _5-2_	weight
coat	slacks	coat _12_	slacks _16_
dress	pajamas	dress _14_	pajamas _36_
suit	bathrobe	suit	bathrobe
sweater	shoes	sweater _Med_	shoes _6½-7_
shirt	hat	shirt	hat _7_
blouse	gloves	blouse _36_	gloves
skirt	ring	skirt _13_	ring _7_

Name _Casey_		Name _Karina_	
height	weight	height	weight
coat _10-12_	slacks _10S_	coat _6_	slacks _6_
dress	pajamas	dress _6_	pajamas
suit	bathrobe	suit	bathrobe
sweater	shoes _1½_	sweater	shoes _11_
shirt _10-12_	hat	shirt	hat
blouse	gloves	blouse _6_	gloves
skirt	ring	skirt	ring

Name		Name	
height	weight	height	weight
coat	slacks	coat	slacks
dress	pajamas	dress	pajamas
suit	bathrobe	suit	bathrobe
sweater	shoes	sweater	shoes
shirt	hat	shirt	hat
blouse	gloves	blouse	gloves
skirt	ring	skirt	ring

Name		Name	
height	weight	height	weight
coat	slacks	coat	slacks
dress	pajamas	dress	pajamas
suit	bathrobe	suit	bathrobe
sweater	shoes	sweater	shoes
shirt	hat	shirt	hat
blouse	gloves	blouse	gloves
skirt	ring	skirt	ring

Holiday Calendar

Monday, November 7

Tuesday, November 1

Tuesday, November 8

Wednesday, November 2

Wednesday, November 9

Thursday, November 3

Thursday, November 10

Friday, November 4

Friday, November 11

Saturday, November 5

Saturday, November 12

Sunday, November 6

Sunday, November 13

Monday, November 14
_____

Tuesday, November 15
_____

Wednesday, November 16
_____

Thursday, November 17
_____

Friday, November 18
_____

Saturday, November 19
_____

Sunday, November 20
_____

_____

Monday, November 21
_____

Tuesday, November 22
_____

Wednesday, November 23
_____

Thursday, November 24
Thanksgiving
_____

Friday, November 25
_____

Saturday, November 26
_____

Sunday, November 27
_____

_____

Monday, November 28

Tuesday, November 29

Wednesday, November 30

Thursday, December 1

Friday, December 2

Saturday, December 3

Sunday, December 4

Monday, December 5

Tuesday, December 6

Wednesday, December 7

Thursday, December 8

Friday, December 9

Saturday, December 10

Sunday, December 11

Monday, December 12

Monday, December 19

Tuesday, December 13

Tuesday, December 20

Wednesday, December 14

Wednesday, December 21

Thursday, December 15

Thursday, December 22

Friday, December 16

Friday, December 23

Saturday, December 17

Saturday, December 24

Sunday, December 18

Sunday, December 25
Christmas

Monday, December 26

Tuesday, December 27

Wednesday, December 28

Thursday, December 29

Friday, December 30

Saturday, December 31

Sunday, January 1
New Year's Day

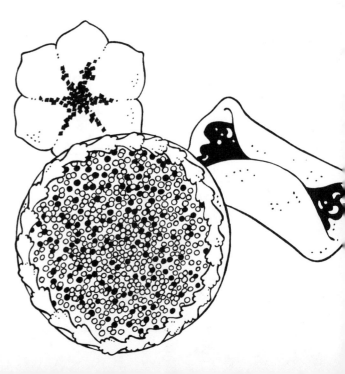

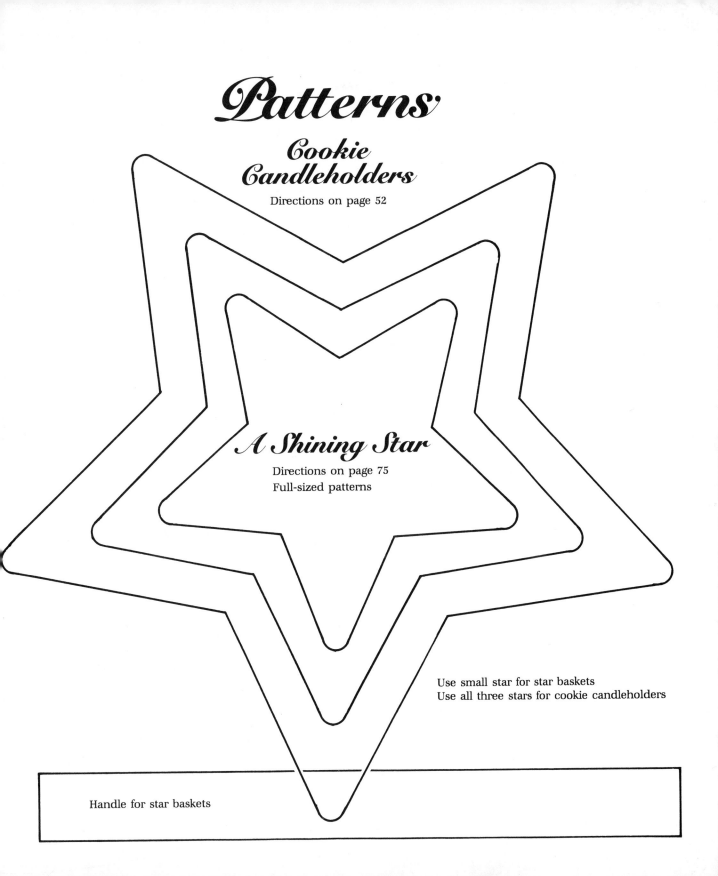

Patterns

Cookie Candleholders

Directions on page 52

A Shining Star

Directions on page 75
Full-sized patterns

Use small star for star baskets
Use all three stars for cookie candleholders

Handle for star baskets

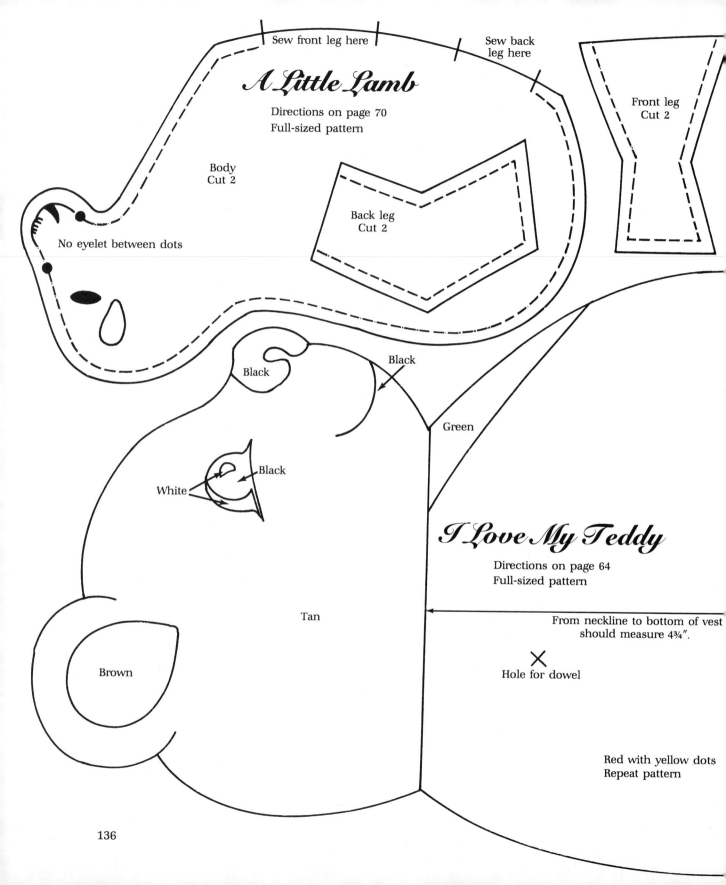

A Little Lamb

Directions on page 70
Full-sized pattern

Sew front leg here

Sew back
leg here

Front leg
Cut 2

Body
Cut 2

No eyelet between dots

Back leg
Cut 2

Black

Black

Green

Black

White

Black

I Love My Teddy

Directions on page 64
Full-sized pattern

Tan

From neckline to bottom of vest
should measure 4¾".

✕
Hole for dowel

Brown

Red with yellow dots
Repeat pattern

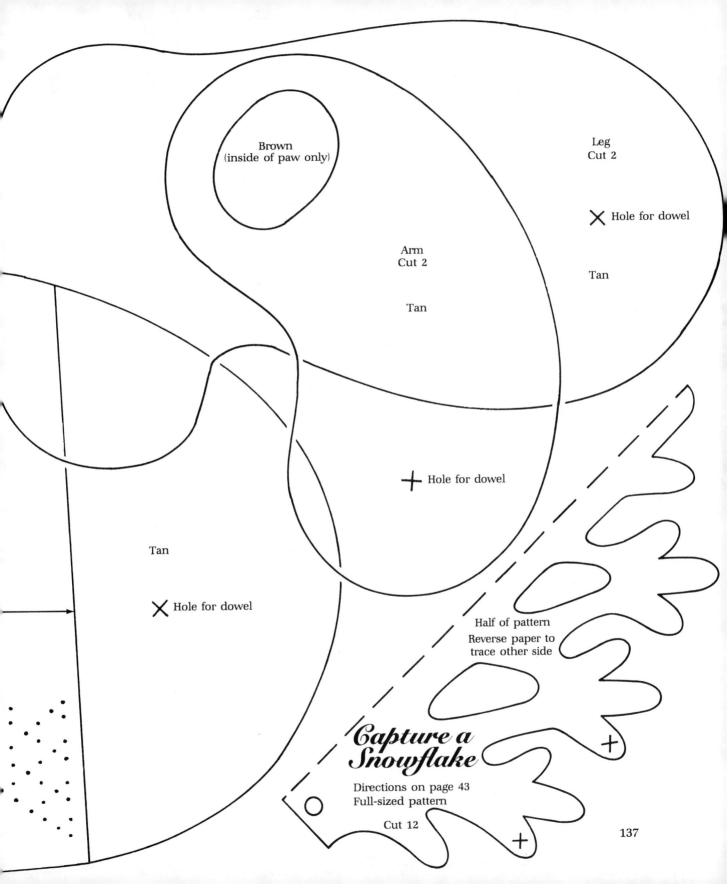

Brown
(inside of paw only)

Leg
Cut 2

✕ Hole for dowel

Arm
Cut 2

Tan

Tan

✚ Hole for dowel

Tan

✕ Hole for dowel

Half of pattern
Reverse paper to
trace other side

*Capture a
Snowflake*

Directions on page 43
Full-sized pattern

Cut 12

137

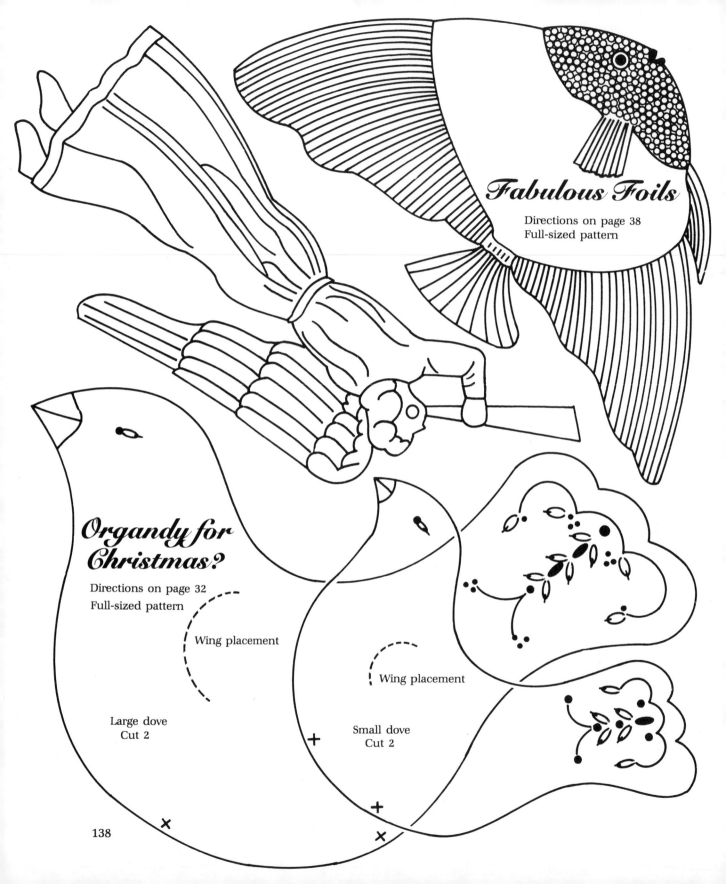

Fabulous Foils

Directions on page 38
Full-sized pattern

Organdy for Christmas?

Directions on page 32
Full-sized pattern

Wing placement

Large dove
Cut 2

Wing placement

Small dove
Cut 2

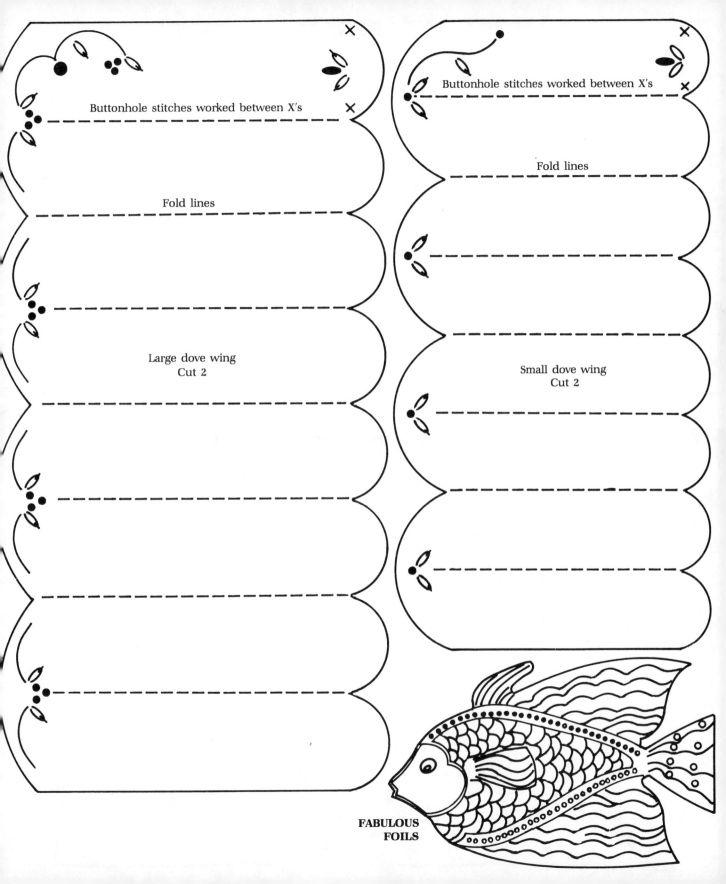

Buttonhole stitches worked between X's

Fold lines

Large dove wing
Cut 2

Buttonhole stitches worked between X's

Fold lines

Small dove wing
Cut 2

FABULOUS FOILS

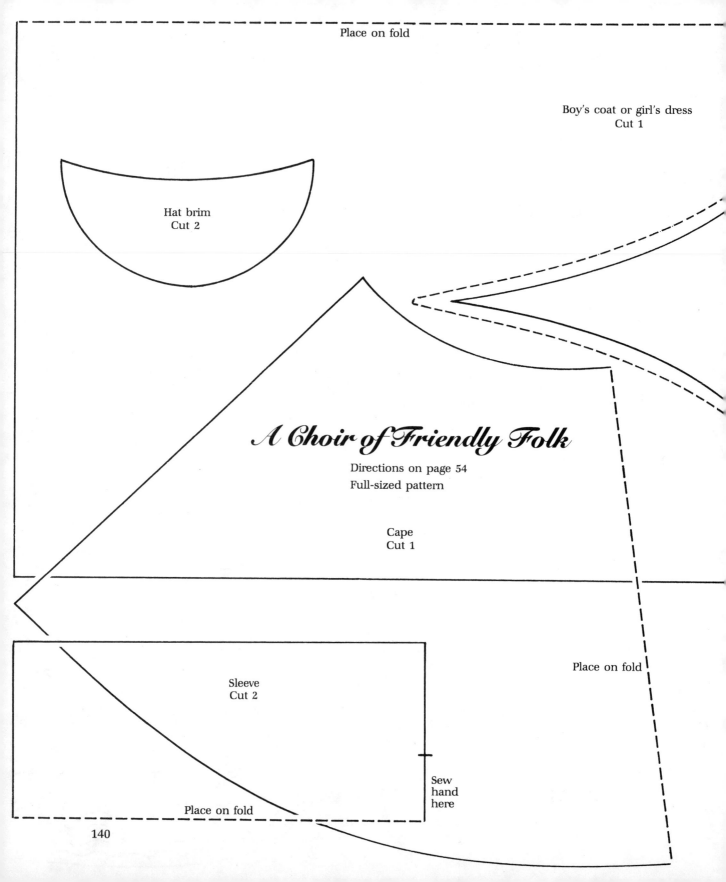

Place on fold

Boy's coat or girl's dress
Cut 1

Hat brim
Cut 2

A Choir of Friendly Folk

Directions on page 54
Full-sized pattern

Cape
Cut 1

Place on fold

Sleeve
Cut 2

Sew
hand
here

Place on fold

140

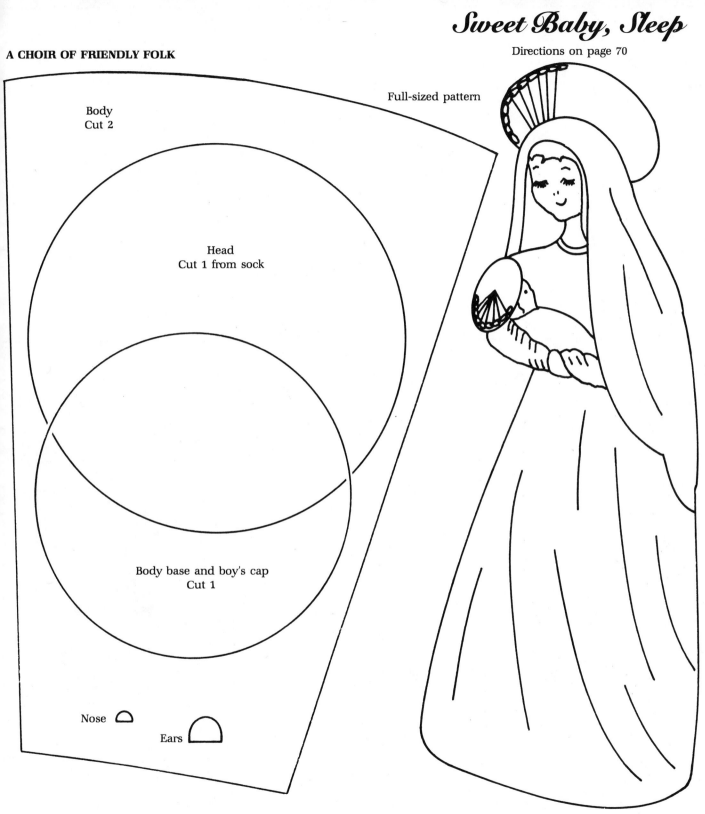

A CHOIR OF FRIENDLY FOLK

Full-sized pattern

Body
Cut 2

Head
Cut 1 from sock

Body base and boy's cap
Cut 1

Nose

Ears

Crocheted Angels

Directions on page 60
Full-sized pattern

Christmas Greetings

Directions on page 59

Band at top
of stocking

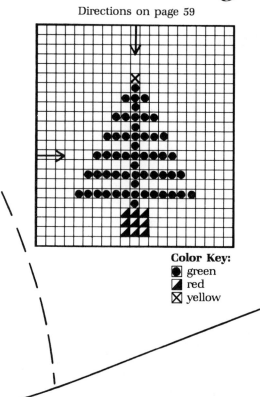

To trace complete stocking pattern, trace foot to top of page. Turn tracing upside down and continue to the top of the stocking. For the dark bands at top of stocking, cut 2 rectangles of medium brown velvet that measure 11½" x 7".

Color Key:
● green
◢ red
☒ yellow

Toe patch
Cut 2 (medium brown)

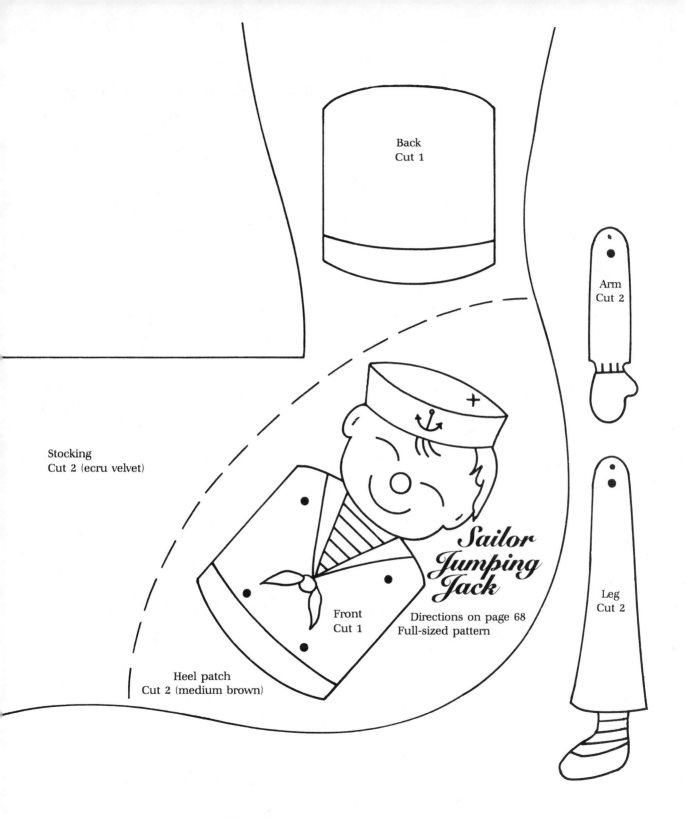

Back
Cut 1

Arm
Cut 2

Stocking
Cut 2 (ecru velvet)

*Sailor
Jumping
Jack*

Directions on page 68
Full-sized pattern

Front
Cut 1

Leg
Cut 2

Heel patch
Cut 2 (medium brown)

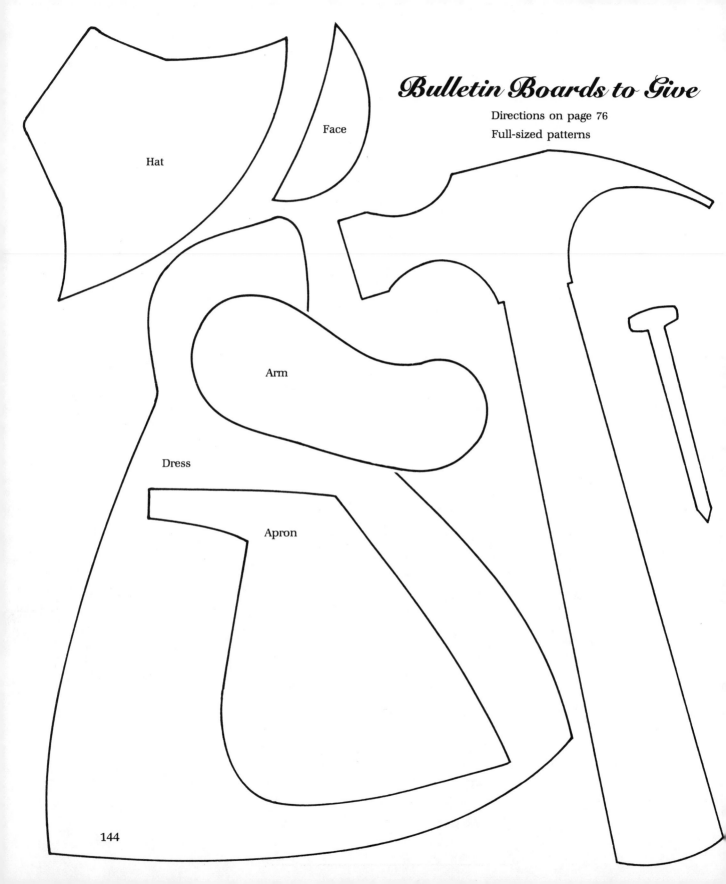

Hat

Face

Bulletin Boards to Give

Directions on page 76

Full-sized patterns

Arm

Dress

Apron

144

Reindeer Parcels

Directions on page 81

Full-sized pattern

A Glint of Gold

Directions on page 58

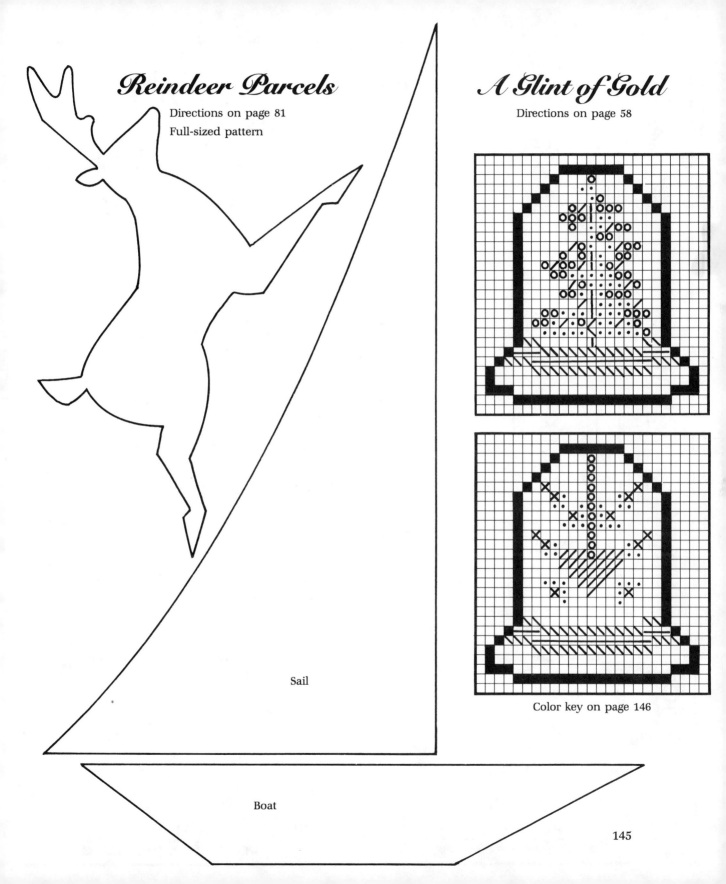

Sail

Boat

Color key on page 146

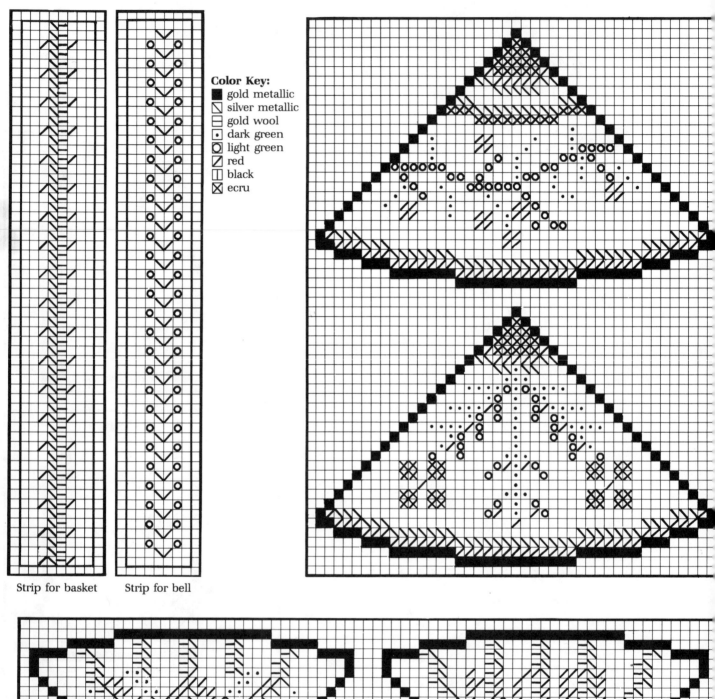

Color Key:

- ■ gold metallic
- ◣ silver metallic
- ⊟ gold wool
- • dark green
- ○ light green
- ◪ red
- ▯ black
- ⊠ ecru

Strip for basket   Strip for bell

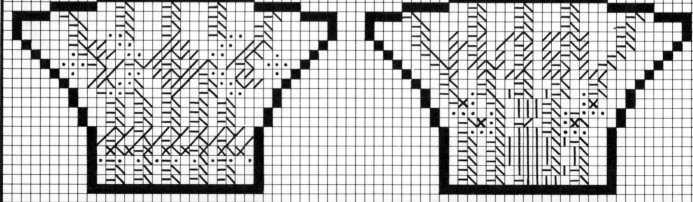

Contributors

Production Editor: Annette Thompson
Editorial Assistant: Patty Howdon
Photo Stylist: Linda M. Stewart
Design: Carol Middleton
Cover Photograph: Charles Walton
Art: Carol Middleton, David Morrison,
 Don Smith
Production: Jerry Higdon

Special thanks to the following people from *Southern Living:* Jean Wickstrom Liles, Foods Editor; Lynn Lloyd, Test Kitchens Director; Beverly Morrow, Foods Photo Stylist; and Vann Cleveland, Director of Photography.

Designers

Lena Anderson, little lamb 70.
Dorinda Beaumont, needlepoint ornaments 58.
Mary Martha Blalock, tree with sweet-grass ornaments 5, low country wreath 18, vine wreaths 67.
Angie Carney, sweet baby sleep 70.
Candace N. Conard, easy accents 44, a touch of glitter 45.
Kay Davis, holiday sachets 63.
Alexandra Eames, golden monograms 39.
Jerry R. Edge, drums 72.
Gerry Hedberg, sailor jumping jack 68.
Dora Hooks, ivy wreath 17, subtle shades of Autumn 49.
Patricia J. Horton, Christmas greetings 59.
Maura C. Kennedy, tree skirt 28.
Posy Baker Lough, small wreaths on curtain rings 66.
Ellen McCarn, decorated cookies on cover, on cookie tree, and throughout the book.
Jeanette B. McCay and Kathryn E. Young, from nature's bounty 16.
Thelma H. McLean, family memory wreath 26.
Carol Middleton, bookmark 77.
David Morrison, snowflake 43, twirler 78.
Sunny O'Neil, Victorian tree under glass 31, moss heart and wreath 48.

Ann Lane Saunderson and Elizabeth L. Wheeler, foil fish and angel 38.
Linda M. Stewart, timeless & simple 34, reflections 36, for a collector 37, quiet tones 45.
Shelley Stewart, organdy baskets 32.
Cameron Ticheli, grandmother's special 56.
Carol M. Tipton, organdy doves 32, choir of friendly folk 54, crocheted angels 60, wooden teddy bear 64.
Jo Voce, felt cookies 27, personal vignette 41, candleholders 52, baskets for bath 79, reindeer parcels 80.
Bob and Sarah Watkins, walk-through wreath 14, pine cone tree 19, toy collection 48.
Sarah, Bob, and Cathy Watkins, walnut ornaments 68.
Rose McLean Whitesides, family memory wreath 25.

Photographers

Jim Bathie, 4, 5, 18, right 37, 52, 66, 67, 68, 69, left 70, 72, 74, 84, 88.
Van Chaplin, 21.
Mary-Gray Hunter, 16, top 34, 41, 42, bottom right 43, 49, bottom 50, 55, 56, 62, 73, left 76.
Louis Joyner, 22, top 23, 47.
Bob Lancaster, 6, top and bottom left 7, top right 9, 46, 51, 82.
Beth Maynor, 10, 11, 17, 24, 27, 28, 29, 30, 32, 33, bottom 34, 35, 36, top left 43, top 45, top 50, 57, 58, 59, 60, 61, 63, right 64, 65, right 70, 71, 75, right 76, 79, 80.
John O'Hagan, 8, 15, 19, 25, 26, 31, 48, left 68, 77, 105, 113.
Gary Parker, 44.
Christina Patoski, bottom left 9.
Bruce Roberts, top and bottom right 7, bottom right 9.
Jody Schwartz, 12.
Shelley Stewart, bottom 23.
Charles E. Walton, cover, title page, 1, 2-3, 13, 38, 39, bottom 45, 53, 83, 85, 93, 96, 102, 108, 116, 121, 123.

147

THE Magazine For You
if You Share Our Interest
in the South.

SOUTHERN LIVING
features articles to help make
life for you and your
family more comfortable,
more stimulating, more fun...

SOUTHERN LIVING is about your home and how to make a
more attractive, more convenient, more comfortable place to
live. Each issue brings you dozens of decorating and remodeling
ideas you can adapt to your own surroundings.

SOUTHERN LIVING is about gardening and landscaping and
how to make the outside of your home just as attractive as the
inside. In addition to gardening features, you'll find a monthly
garden calendar pinpointing what to plant and when, plus a
"Letters to our Garden Editor" section to answer your own
particular questions.

SOUTHERN LIVING is about good food and entertaining, with
recipes and menu ideas that are sure to delight your family and
friends. You'll discover recipes with a Southern accent from
some of the South's superlative cooks.

SOUTHERN LIVING is about travel and just plain fun. Every
new issue offers an information-packed monthly calendar of
special events and happenings throughout the South, plus
features on the many facinating places of interest the South has
to offer.

To find out how you can receive SOUTHERN LIVING every
month, simply write to: SOUTHERN LIVING, P. O. Box
C-119, Birmingham, AL 35283.